SAM'S EATS

SAM'S EATS

LET'S DO
SOME
COOKING

SAM WAY

VORACIOUS

LITTLE, BROWN AND COMPANY
NEW YORK   BOSTON   LONDON

Voracious / Little, Brown and Company
Hachette Book Group
1290 Avenue of the Americas, New York, NY 10104
voraciousbooks.com

First North American edition: November 2023
Originally published in the United Kingdom by Seven Oaks, a division of the Orion Publishing Group, Ltd., September 2023.

Voracious is an imprint of Little, Brown and Company, a division of Hachette Book Group, Inc. The Voracious name and logo are trademarks of Hachette Book Group, Inc.

The publisher is not responsible for websites (or their content) that are not owned by the publisher.

The Hachette Speakers Bureau provides a wide range of authors for speaking events. To find out more, go to hachettespeakersbureau.com or email HachetteSpeakers@hbgusa.com.

Little, Brown and Company books may be purchased in bulk for business, educational, or promotional use. For information, please contact your local bookseller or the Hachette Book Group Special Markets Department at special.markets@hbgusa.com.

Photographs by David Loftus

ISBN 9780316566872
Library of Congress Control Number is available from the publisher.

10 9 8 7 6 5 4 3 2 1

MOHN

Printed in Germany

To my wonderful family, girlfriend and friends x

CONTENTS

INTRODUCTION

My love for food has been with me for as long as I can remember.

I was lucky enough to grow up in a household surrounded by delicious home-cooked meals; one that celebrated good ingredients and the whole process of cooking. This made me keen to get into the kitchen myself and see where the creative process could take me. I was constantly curious as to how things were made and where they came from and, naturally, this paved the way for where I am today.

My career in the food and drink industry didn't start in the typical way, to say the least. While playing sport at school, I sustained a head injury which had a significant impact on both my physical and mental health; I really struggled to focus and find the drive I once had. My dream of turning my skill and passion for sport into a full-time career was derailed, leaving me feeling lost and confused with where I wanted to go. As a result, I left school without my A levels (for my American audience, this is the last two years of high school) in the hope I'd figure everything out.

Over the next few years, I spent time going between various things, from working as a waiter to running my own business and travelling. Throughout this time, I never felt truly settled and happy, and all the while I saw my peers striding ahead in their lives, making their way to university or starting careers in the professional world of work.

Since the day I got injured, the one thing that had always given me a buzz, purpose and escape in life, and made me incredibly happy, was cooking. Whether that was making food for family and friends, and sharing wonderful memories and moments around the dinner table, or spending time discovering new foods, cuisines and recipes through personal research and travelling, I was always left with an overwhelmingly positive feeling.

It was after leaving an unfulfilling job a few years later that I asked myself the question, 'What really brings me the most joy in life?'

Quickly realising it was cooking and food, I knew that I had to get myself into the industry to do something that would be sustainable and fruitful.

With this in mind, my first port of call was to look for work in a kitchen or small food and drink start-up. To do this, I knew I needed to gain some experience first. Of course, going in at an entry level job and 'working my way up' was the obvious option. However, it was midway through the second wave of Covid and the hospitality industry and small businesses were struggling and people were losing their jobs left, right and centre. I felt that I needed to bring something more to the table to be in with the chance of securing a position. It was then that I decided to set up social media as a specific space to build a digital portfolio for my cooking. I could then use this to approach companies and kitchens, to show them how passionate I really was. I hadn't intended for my videos to be seen and enjoyed by anyone other than those who I was going to reach out to for work.

Things took an unexpected turn, though, and within a few weeks of starting my page, my videos were getting hundreds of thousands of views and my followings were growing rapidly across all platforms. It was then that I realised that I might not need to stick to my original plan of working in a kitchen or joining a small business, but instead, maybe, just maybe, I could start something of my own. I had always wanted to pave my own way in life and build a business, so now felt like the perfect opportunity to do so.

Being part of an online community and support system is an incredible thing. It gives me the confidence and drive to keep trying new things, really listen to what my audience want, and push the boundaries with food and flavour. Every day I look to inspire people to get into the kitchen and create great-tasting food with confidence and excitement. My love for food and cooking is central to my life and if I can help just one person feel that joy when they cook, then mission accomplished.

Fast forward to now – I am sitting here in awe of how incredible this journey has been. While I love creating content online, I wanted to look at different ways to spread my passion for food. Writing a cookbook seemed like the perfect next step. The whole process of creating this book has been an amazing journey, from researching and writing to developing and shooting the recipes with a wonderful team. It has been an incredible experience, and one that I will hopefully get to have again soon.

So, what can you expect from this book? I am a home-cook at heart, so I've written this book with all of you home-cooks in mind. Inside is a selection of what I believe are some of the most delicious homemade meals; food that people want to eat, food that people want to make – and *can* make – and, most importantly, food that will bring people together and help create wonderful memories. With my constant enthusiasm for researching food from different cultures, paired with the travelling I have done and tasting much that the cuisines have to offer, this book contains influences from around the world. There is so much incredible flavour out there to be appreciated that it's hard not to want to share it.

The book is made up of various chapters that cover recipes for all skill levels, whether a beginner or a keen home-cook, and includes a range of recipes for different occasions. Whether you are looking for an easy after-work dish to cook up quickly midweek, or you're wanting to put on a show-stopping spread for your friends and family at the weekend, there will be something for everyone.

If there are three things that I urge you to take away from this book, they are to *enjoy* the process of cooking, *relish* the feeling of creating something beautiful and *love* the result of creating happy memories with those around you.

Let's do some cooking!

Sam

HOW TO USE THIS BOOK

If you're someone who likes to follow instructions to the letter, then you'll be guaranteed a delicious dish every time. However, if you are a more experimental cook, feel free to use the recipes as a guide, incorporating your own twists and preferences. As long as you follow the key technical aspects of the recipes, this won't be a problem. One piece of advice – taste the food as you go! Check for seasoning throughout the process and adjust according to your taste. In my opinion, you should use enough salt to enhance and bring out all the wonderful flavours from the ingredients.

I've split the book into six chapters to cater for different occasions.

Brunch

These dishes are aimed at the weekends when you have a bit more time on your hands. However, recipes such as the granola can be prepared in bulk, split into batches and used throughout the week as a quick, hassle-free and tasty breakfast.

Weeknight Meals

These recipes are for those occasions when you finish a long day at work and you're looking to cook something quickly and easily, without sacrificing any of the wonderful flavours we all want from our food.

Quick Prep, Slow Cook

This is a very versatile chapter. The idea behind these recipes is that they take very little time to prepare, but are left to cook for an extended period. This is one of my favourite ways to cook, as it requires very little effort to create a stunning meal.

All Out

These are the showstopper recipes in the book. When you have a bit more time on your hands, or are looking to get immersed in some cooking, this is the chapter for you.

Sharing Plates

The perfect dishes for when you're cooking for lots of people. These sharing plates are a great way to cater for friends or family, and they all work well as part of a spread.

Sides & Salads

This chapter has a multitude of recipes that all pair nicely with other dishes in the book. If you are stuck for what to eat alongside your main meal, you'll find lots of tasty options here.

Sweet Treats

This will be the highlight chapter for those with a sweet tooth. I've included recipes that vary in difficulty and length of time to prepare, so there's something for every occasion.

MADE FROM SCRATCH

You'll find double-page spreads scattered throughout the book that show you how to make certain foods from scratch – the 'Made From Scratch' pages. These are recipes that will make a huge difference to your cooking.

All the 'Made From Scratch' recipes are linked to one or two other dishes in the book and I'd highly recommend giving them all a try. Not only are they delicious, but they are great skills to learn in the kitchen and are very fulfilling once made.

Corn Tortillas & Tostadas
Made very simply with just three ingredients, these are so much better than the shop-bought kind. Use them for Huevos Rancheros (see pages 30–1), Birria Bowls (see page 97), Mushroom, Fish or Steak Tacos (see pages 121–5) and Chicken Fajitas (see page 133).

Fresh Pasta Dough
Once you've mastered the art of making fresh pasta, you can use it to replace dried varieties for all the pasta dishes in the book – use it for the Pea & Mint Rigatoni (see page 42), Roasted Cherry Tomato Cavatappi (see page 45), Creamy Sausage & Mushroom Pasta (see page 50), Crab Linguine (see page 67), Mushroom Ragù (see page 84), Ribeye Ragù (see page 88) and Courgette & Lemon Tortellini (see page 140).

Greek-style Pittas
This recipe not only makes fantastic pittas but the dough can be used as the base for all kinds of flatbreads. Serve these pittas alongside Prawn Saganaki (see page 60), with Peri Peri Chicken (see page 76), Chicken Gyros (see page 102) and Adana Kebab (see page 106), or roll them out more thinly to make French Onion Flatbreads (see page 165).

Japanese Milk Bread Burger Buns
This recipe makes the ultimate bun for a burger, or for any other dish when you need bread that is fluffy and delicious. Japanese milk bread is soft, chewy and full of flavour.

Chai-spiced Custard
This takes custard to a whole new level. Serve alongside the Raspberry Soufflés (see page 208), Chocolate & Pistachio Fondant (see page 212), Apple & Pear Crumble (see page 223) or Sticky Toffee Pudding (see page 224).

PB & J BRIOCHE FRENCH TOAST/18

MAPLE, BACON & PECAN PANCAKES/21

HOMEMADE GRANOLA/22

HARISSA SCRAMBLED EGGS/25

TURKISH EGGS/26

CORN TORTILLAS & TOSTADAS/29

HUEVOS RANCHEROS/31

SWEET POTATO HASH/34

SHAKSHUKA/35

THE ULTIMATE GRILLED CHEESE/37

SMOKED SALMON LATKE/38

BRUNCH

01

PB & J BRIOCHE FRENCH TOAST

PB & J is a classic combination that never fails to please. Adding these flavours to the inside of your French toast takes it to a whole new level. Feel free to serve this with extra peanut butter and strawberry compote drizzled over the top.

MAKES 2 LARGE PORTIONS, WITH SOME COMPOTE LEFT OVER

2 large eggs
200ml (scant 1 cup) whole milk
2 tsp vanilla extract
4 tsp honey
2 slices of brioche bread (or any soft white bread), 3cm (1¼inch) thick (see Note below)
2 tbsp strawberry compote (see recipe below), plus extra for topping
2 tbsp smooth peanut butter, softened in a microwave or over a bain marie, plus extra for topping
Knob of butter (about 2 tbsp)
Icing (confectioner's) sugar, for dusting

For the strawberry compote
350g (12oz) frozen strawberries
60g (¼ cup) caster (superfine) sugar
Small pinch of flaky sea salt
2 tbsp lemon juice

Notes: Make sure to use bread with a very soft crust – this makes it easier to cut a pocket.

A quick hack for making a piping bag is to cut the corner off a plastic Ziplock bag.

1 For the strawberry compote, add all the ingredients to a pan and cook over a medium heat for 15–20 minutes, or until the strawberries have broken down and the sauce has thickened. Use a spoon to break down any of the larger strawberries. Remove from the heat and leave to cool.

2 In a wide and shallow dish, beat the egg with the milk, vanilla extract and honey.

3 Using a knife, cut a slit along the bottom crust of each slice of bread and up through the slice, to create a pocket for the filling.

4 Using a piping (pastry) bag, pipe 1 tablespoon of the compote into the middle of each slice of bread, followed by 1 tablespoon of peanut butter. If you don't have a piping bag, use a spoon to add the filling (also see Note below).

5 Place the stuffed slices into the egg and milk mixture, then leave to soak for 5 minutes on each side so they absorb the liquid.

6 Melt the butter in a large nonstick frying pan over a medium heat, then fry the bread on each side for 7–8 minutes, until browned and cooked through.

7 Remove from the heat, dust with icing sugar and spoon over some more compote and peanut butter to serve.

MAPLE, BACON & PECAN PANCAKES

This is my go-to recipe for fluffy pancakes every time. Making a maple, bacon and pecan crumb means you get some of those flavours in every single bite.

**SERVES 4
(MAKES 12 PANCAKES)**

500g (1lb 2oz) plain (all-purpose) flour
2 tsp baking powder
½ tsp bicarbonate of soda (baking soda)
1 tsp fine sea salt
70g (⅓ cup) caster (superfine) sugar
3 large eggs
70g (2½oz) butter, melted and slightly cooled, plus 4 small knobs (about 1 tsp each) to finish (optional)
60ml (¼ cup) whole milk
600ml (2⅔ cups) buttermilk
1 tsp vanilla extract
Oil spray, for frying

For the bacon, pecan and maple crumb
160g (5½oz) bacon lardons
75g (¾ cup) pecans
3 tbsp maple syrup, plus extra for topping

1   To make the bacon, pecan and maple crumb, add the lardons to a cold frying pan and place over a medium heat until crispy and all the fat has rendered, about 15 minutes. Remove from the pan and place onto kitchen paper to soak up any excess fat, so they stay crispy.

2   To the same pan, add the pecans and toast for 5 minutes, making sure not to burn them. Remove the nuts to a chopping board with the bacon and roughly chop it all into a crumb. Tip into a bowl and mix with the maple syrup. Set aside.

3   In a large bowl, whisk together the flour, baking powder, bicarb, salt and sugar.

4   Whisk the eggs, melted butter, milk, buttermilk and vanilla extract in a separate bowl, then pour the wet ingredients into the dry ingredients and mix until combined. Don't overmix the batter – some lumps are ok. Expect the batter to be thick – this helps with the shape and fluffiness of the pancakes.

5   Spray some oil into a nonstick frying pan and place over a medium-low heat. Once up to temperature, add some batter to the pan and cook 3 or 4 pancakes at a time for 3–4 minutes on each side until browned.

6   Transfer to a plate, cover with foil and place in a low temperature oven while you cook the rest of the pancakes, adding oil spray to the frying pan as needed. Keep the pancakes covered in foil for around 10 minutes, which will allow them to continue steaming, ensuring they are fully cooked through and fluffy.

7   Place the pancakes on plates and top with a small knob of butter, if you like. Add a drizzle of maple syrup and spoon over some crumb to serve.

HOMEMADE GRANOLA

Making granola at home is easy, cost effective and incredibly tasty. I like to make a big batch and store it in an airtight container for a few weeks. It really is the perfect hassle-free breakfast for a busy week.

MAKES 7–8 PORTIONS

100g (⅔ cup) dates, finely chopped
50g (⅓ cup) sultanas (golden raisins)
50g (2½ tbsp) honey
50g (2½ tbsp) unsalted butter
60g (⅓ cup) soft brown sugar
2 egg whites
200g (2¼ cups) porridge (rolled) oats
150g (1½ cups) pecans, roughly chopped
Pinch of sea salt
1 tsp ground cinnamon
¼ tsp ground ginger

1 Preheat the oven to 150°C (300°F) Gas Mark 2 and line a baking tray with baking parchment.

2 Tip the dates and sultanas into a bowl and add boiling water to cover. Leave to soak while you prepare the remaining ingredients.

3 Place the honey, butter and sugar in a saucepan and cook over a low heat until the sugar has dissolved, stirring frequently.

4 In a bowl, whisk the egg whites until frothy and doubled in volume.

5 Drain the soaked fruits.

6 Place the oats, drained fruits, pecans, salt, cinnamon, ginger and melted butter mixture in a large bowl. Mix together until combined, then add the whisked egg whites and mix again until they have all been incorporated.

7 Spread the granola out on the prepared baking tray and cook in the oven for 35 minutes until golden and crisp. Halfway through cooking, crumble up the granola a bit and give it a mix so more sides can brown.

8 Once cooked and golden brown, remove the granola from the oven and leave to cool.

9 Serve with some thick Greek yogurt and honey. Store in an airtight jar for 1–2 weeks.

HARISSA SCRAMBLED EGGS

The key to great scrambled eggs is time – cook them slowly over a low heat and you'll always end up with the softest eggs. The harissa and sour cream take it to a whole new dimension, with minimal effort, making the eggs even more silky and flavoursome. If you can't get hold of rose harissa, regular harissa will work too.

SERVES 2

5 large eggs
Knob of butter (about 2 tbsp)
2 tsp rose harissa paste
2 tsp soured cream
2–4 slices of sourdough bread,
   toasted and buttered

To finish
2 tsp rose harissa paste
1 tbsp olive oil
Small bunch of chives, finely
   chopped

1   Crack the eggs into a bowl and beat well. Tip them into a cold saucepan with the knob of butter.

2   Place the pan over a medium-low heat and cook the eggs for 10–15 minutes, until silky-smooth but slightly thick (you can't have them too soft, as adding the sour cream later will thin them out a bit). For best results, take it slowly, continuously stirring so the eggs don't stick to the bottom of the pan and overcook. For me, there is nothing worse than overcooked chunks of egg – if you feel the eggs getting too hot, remove the pan from the heat for a few seconds, while stirring, to let it cool down slightly.

3   Once cooked, season with sea salt and freshly ground black pepper, add the harissa paste and soured cream and mix well until all incorporated.

4   Mix the harissa paste with the olive oil.

5   Serve the eggs on the toasted sourdough, drizzle over the harissa oil and top with a sprinkling of chives.

TURKISH EGGS

This has to be one of my absolute favourite breakfasts. Turkish eggs, known as *cilbir*, always go down a treat. How do you eat this? Cut open the runny poached eggs and scoop up the yolk with some yoghurt using the buttery toasted sourdough.

SERVES 4

2 tbsp white vinegar
8 large eggs
Squeeze of lemon juice
4 slices of sourdough bread,
    toasted and buttered

For the yogurt
300g (1⅓ cups) Greek yogurt
Grated zest of 1 lemon
Small bunch of dill, finely chopped,
    plus extra to garnish

For the spiced garlic butter
40g (3 tbsp) butter
3 garlic cloves, sliced
1 tsp dried chilli flakes
1 tsp ground cumin
1 tsp smoked paprika
Pinch of sea salt
Small bunch of parsley, finely
    chopped, plus extra to garnish

Note: You can try to cook more eggs at one time, but I find that with more than 4, the egg whites start sticking together.

1   Mix together the yogurt, lemon zest and dill, and season with sea salt. Set aside.

2   Add all the ingredients for the spiced garlic butter, except the parsley, to a pan. Place over a low heat and cook for 8–10 minutes, until the garlic has started to brown and is fragrant.

3   While the butter is cooking, bring a deep pan of water to a simmer, add the vinegar, then stir the water in a circular motion to make a whirlpool. With the water still moving, swiftly crack the eggs into the water, in batches of 4 (see Note below). Cook for 3 minutes, if using room temperature eggs, or 3½ minutes for fridge-cold eggs, to get the perfect runny yolk. Lift the eggs out of the water with a slotted spoon and place on some kitchen paper to soak up any excess water.

4   Once the butter has melted and infused, remove from the heat, stir in the parsley.

5   Spoon the yogurt onto a serving plate and smooth it out with the back of the spoon. Place the poached eggs on top of the yogurt, then drizzle over the spiced garlic butter. Garnish with some sprigs of dill and parsley leaves, and squeeze over some lemon juice. Serve with the buttered sourdough toast.

MADE FROM SCRATCH
CORN TORTILLAS & TOSTADAS

Making corn tortillas from scratch is a lot easier than you might think. Be sure to use masa harina flour. This differs from regular corn flour as it has undergone a process called nixtamalization, which makes it easier to work with and more nutritious. Try a brand called Maseca, which can be ordered online.

MAKES 16

240g (8½oz) masa harina flour
½ tsp fine sea salt
330ml (1½ cups) hot water

You will need
2 sheets of plastic (cut the top off a
   Ziplock bag, then cut it in half)
Tortilla press or heavy-based pan

Note: Step 4 is a trick I learnt while in Mexico, and it makes a huge difference. If you make sure to loosen the top layer of plastic, as explained there, you will have no problem peeling off the tortilla once pressed, and it is far less likely to rip or tear.

Vegetable oil, for frying
Cooked corn tortillas (see above)

CORN TORTILLAS

1 Add the flour and salt to a bowl. Gradually pour in the water while mixing with a spoon. Once all the water has been incorporated, bring the dough together with your hands and tip out onto a clean work surface.

2 Gently knead the dough for 30 seconds until it comes together and is smooth. Place it back in the bowl, cover with a damp tea (dish) towel and leave to sit for 30 minutes so the flour can completely hydrate. If you don't do this, you will notice the edges of the tortilla crack.

3 Divide the dough into 16 balls, keeping them covered with the tea towel. Place a ball between 2 pieces of plastic, place in a tortilla press, or underneath a heavy pan on a flat surface. Press down until flattened.

4 Carefully peel off the top layer of plastic to loosen it and make it easier to remove later. Lay it back on top of the tortilla, then flip over on to the other side. Press down again, then gently peel the plastic off the tortilla.

5 In batches, lay the tortillas in a hot, dry frying pan over a medium-high heat. Cook for 15 seconds on the first side, flip over and cook for 45 seconds, then flip again and cook for a final 45 seconds. If the tortillas are slightly thicker, you may need to cook them for 1 minute on each side.

6 Once cooked, remove the tortillas from the pan and wrap in a tea towel. Place the wrapped tortilla bundle into a saucepan and cover with a lid. This allows them to steam and will soften them further, ready for eating.

TOSTADAS

1 Heat a 2.5cm (1-inch) depth of vegetable oil in a sauté pan over a medium-high heat.

2 Once hot, fry the tortillas in the oil, in batches, for a few minutes until golden and crisp. Remove from the heat, place on some kitchen paper to soak up any excess oil and sprinkle with sea salt.

HUEVOS RANCHEROS

This recipe is my version of a Mexican classic. Crispy tostadas drenched in salsas and topped with refried beans and fried eggs – you just can't go wrong! Especially when paired with black coffee.

SERVES 4–6

4–6 tostadas (see page 29)
4–6 fried eggs

To serve, place a tostada onto a plate, top with some refried beans and a fried egg, spoon over some salsa roja, then serve the pico de gallo and avocado, feta and mint on the side.

REFRIED BEANS

1 tbsp olive oil
1 onion, finely chopped
2 garlic cloves, grated
2 tsp cumin seeds
1 tsp ground coriander
2 x 400g (14oz) cans of black beans, drained and rinsed
150ml (⅔ cup) vegetable stock
Small bunch of coriander (cilantro), finely chopped
Juice of 1 lime

1 Heat the oil in a saucepan over a medium heat. Add the onion and fry for 5–6 minutes until soft and translucent. Add the garlic and fry for another 2 minutes, then stir in the cumin and coriander and cook for 1 more minute.

2 Add the black beans and stock and season with sea salt and freshly ground black pepper.

3 Cook over a medium-low heat for 15–20 minutes until the beans are very soft.

4 Mash with a fork until a thicker sauce is formed. If it's too runny, cook for a few more minutes to evaporate any excess water. Stir in the chopped coriander and lime juice, and check for seasoning.

PICO DE GALLO

4 vine tomatoes, deseeded and finely diced
1 fresh jalapeño chilli, finely diced
½ white onion, finely diced
Small bunch of coriander (cilantro), leaves finely chopped
Juice of 1 lime

1 Mix all the ingredients together in a bowl and season with sea salt to taste. Set aside until ready to use.

SALSA ROJA

6 plum tomatoes, halved
1 onion, peeled and quartered
2 fresh jalapeño chillies
4 garlic cloves, peeled
Small bunch of coriander (cilantro),
    stalks removed and leaves finely
    chopped
1 tbsp olive oil

1 Preheat the oven to 200°C (400°F) Gas Mark 6 and the grill (broiler) to high.

2 Lay the tomatoes, onion, jalapeños and garlic on a baking tray lined with baking parchment and place under the grill for 5–6 minutes until everything has a slight char.

3 Remove from the grill, take out the garlic and set aside, then roast the rest of the vegetables in the oven for 20 minutes.

4 Once cooked, place the roasted vegetables and garlic in a blender. Briefly blitz everything together, but not for too long as we still want some texture. Tip the salsa out into a bowl, add the coriander and olive oil, season with sea salt and mix together well before serving.

AVOCADO, FETA & MINT

2 ripe avocados, finely chopped
Handful of mint leaves, finely
    chopped
2 tbsp olive oil
100g (scant 1 cup) crumbled feta
Squeeze of lemon juice

1 Add the avocados, mint, olive oil and feta to a bowl. Squeeze over some lemon juice, season with sea salt and mix together.

SWEET POTATO HASH

This is a very simple dish, but the sweetness of the potato and the saltiness of the feta work particularly well together. It is one of those fuss-free recipes where you can chuck everything into the pan and let it cook away. A big bowl of this on a Sunday morning with a fried egg on top is a win-win.

SERVES 2–3

2 tbsp olive oil

1 white onion, diced

1 medium-sized sweet potato, peeled and cut into small cubes (300–350g/10½–12oz prepared weight)

3 garlic cloves, sliced

2 tbsp water

40g (1½oz) kale, large stalks removed

Small bunch of parsley, leaves finely chopped

100g (scant 1 cup) crumbled feta

2–3 large eggs

1   Heat half the oil in a sauté pan over a medium heat. Add the onion and sweet potato, and season with sea salt and freshly ground black pepper. Fry for 10 minutes until softened and starting to caramelize, then add the garlic and water and cook for another 5 minutes.

2   Add the kale, parsley and feta, cover with a lid and cook for 10 minutes until the sweet potato has softened and the feta has melted.

3   Meanwhile, add the remaining oil to a frying pan over a medium-high heat. Crack in the eggs and fry for 5 minutes until the whites have cooked.

4   Serve the sweet potato hash in bowls, with a fried egg over the top.

SHAKSHUKA

It seems that most cookbooks nowadays include a version of shakshuka, and this is for a good reason – it's easy to make and delicious! The secret to a great shakshuka is to let the tomatoes cook down until thickened and rich in flavour. From there, whether you follow this recipe to a tee or adjust it to your preference, you're on track for a guaranteed tasty breakfast.

SERVES 4

2 tbsp olive oil, plus extra to finish
3 shallots, finely chopped
3 garlic cloves, finely sliced
1 red chilli, deseeded and finely chopped
2 tsp smoked paprika
4 cardamom pods, seeds removed and crushed
1 tsp ground cumin
1 x 400g (14oz) can of cannellini beans, drained and rinsed
1 x 400g (14oz) can of chopped tomatoes
100g (3½oz) baby leaf spinach
150ml (⅔ cup) water
4 large eggs
Small bunch of coriander (cilantro), leaves only
4 slices of sourdough bread, toasted and buttered

1   Heat the oil in a frying pan, add the shallots and fry for 5 minutes over a medium heat.

2   Season with salt, then add the garlic and chilli and fry for a few more minutes.

3   Stir in the spices and cook for 1 minute, then add the beans, tomatoes, spinach and water. Cover with a lid and cook for 15–20 minutes.

4   Make 4 deep wells in the shakshuka and crack an egg into each one. Cover with a lid and cook for 4–5 minutes, until the whites have just set – make sure you don't overcook the eggs here, as it's easily done.

5   Remove the shakshuka from the heat, top with coriander leaves, a drizzle of oil and some flaky sea salt and freshly ground black pepper. Serve with toasted sourdough, slathered with butter.

THE ULTIMATE GRILLED CHEESE

This is one of the more indulgent brunch dishes in this chapter. The combination of salty and sharp cheeses with the rich and sweet caramelized onions and pears is a fantastic combination. This can be eaten on its own, but also works well when served with a bitter leaf salad or a bowl of soup.

SERVES 2

50g (2oz) mature Cheddar, grated
50g (2oz) shredded mozzarella
50g (2oz) Gruyère, grated
4 large slices of sourdough bread
3 tbsp unsalted butter, softened
Drizzle of olive oil

For the caramelized onions
1 tbsp truffle oil
Large knob of unsalted butter
  (about 2 tbsp)
2 medium onions, finely sliced
1 pear, peeled, cored and finely
  diced
2 tbsp whisky (optional, but adds a
  lovely smokiness) OR beef stock
1 tsp balsamic vinegar
1 tsp Dijon mustard
Few sprigs of thyme, leaves only

1 Heat the truffle oil and butter in a frying pan over a medium heat, then add the onions and pear. Fry for 10–15 minutes until soft and starting to caramelize.

2 Deglaze the pan with the whisky (or stock) and allow most of it to evaporate. Add the balsamic vinegar, mustard and thyme leaves, and season with sea salt and freshly ground black pepper to taste, bearing in mind the cheeses will be salty. Cook for a further 5–10 minutes, stirring frequently until the onions and pear have turned a rich golden brown. Remove from the heat and set aside.

3 Preheat the oven to 180°C (350°F) Gas Mark 4.

4 Mix the cheeses together in a bowl.

5 Butter each slice of bread on one side then flip them over (this is important as you want the buttered sides facing outwards when you fry the sandwich). Sprinkle half the cheese onto one unbuttered side of bread, spreading it out to the edges. Spread 2 tablespoons of caramelized onions onto another slice of bread then sandwich them together. Repeat this step for the other sandwich.

6 Heat a drizzle of oil in an ovenproof frying pan over a medium heat, then add the sandwiches. Cook on each side for 3–4 minutes, flipping halfway through, until both sides are golden brown. Place the pan in the oven for 5 minutes, to ensure all of the cheese has melted.

7 Take the pan out of the oven, remove the toastie, cut in half and serve immediately while the cheese is oozy and hot.

SMOKED SALMON LATKE

This is my twist on a Jewish latke. By turning this into one large latke, it works as a sharing platter and is a huge crowd pleaser. If you want to go a step further, feel free to add a runny poached egg on top.

SERVES 4

For the latke
400g (14oz) potatoes
½ large onion, grated
1 large egg
30g (¼ cup) cornflour (cornstarch)
3 garlic cloves, minced
Sprig of rosemary, needles finely chopped
3 tbsp olive oil

For the topping
85g (generous ⅓ cup) sour cream
1 tbsp finely chopped dill, plus extra sprigs to garnish
1 tsp honey
1 tsp wholegrain mustard
Grated zest of 1 lemon
100g (3½oz) smoked salmon

Note: A foolproof way of flipping the latke is to place a plate on top of the frying pan, holding it securely with one hand, and quickly turn it upside down. Then, simply slide the latke back into the frying pan to continue.

1 To make the latke, peel then grate the potatoes. Rinse them in a bowl of cold water to remove the excess starch. Rinse one more time, then place in a tea (dish) towel with the onion and squeeze out as much of the moisture as possible.

2 Tip the potato and onion into a new bowl and add the egg, cornflour, garlic, rosemary and sea salt and freshly ground black pepper to taste. Mix thoroughly.

3 Add the olive oil to a frying pan and heat to medium-high. Tip in the potato mixture and press down so it spreads out fully to the edges. Fry for 7–8 minutes, until golden and crisp, then flip the latke over and fry for another 7–8 minutes, until the second side is crisp and golden as well (see Note).

4 While the latke is cooking, mix together the sour cream, chopped dill, honey, mustard and lemon zest, with sea salt to taste.

5 When the latke is ready to serve, slide it out onto a board and top with some dollops of sour cream, torn pieces of smoked salmon and a sprinkling of dill. Cut into wedges to serve.

PEA & MINT RIGATONI/42

ROASTED CHERRY TOMATO CAVATAPPI/45

TARRAGON CHICKEN/46

HERBY BREADCRUMB SALMON TRAYBAKE/49

CREAMY SAUSAGE & MUSHROOM PASTA/50

TAMARIND & COCONUT CAULIFLOWER STEAKS/52

PORK CHOPS WITH CHIMICHURRI/53

SPICY TORTILLA/56

MUSHROOM RISOTTO/59

PRAWN SAGANAKI/60

SPICED CAULIFLOWER SOUP/63

GNOCCHI CARBONARA/64

CRAB LINGUINE/67

BUTTERNUT SQUASH ORZO/68

CRISPY CHICKPEA DAL/69

ITALIAN-STYLE MEATBALLS/71

CHICKEN ADOBO/72

PANEER BUTTER MASALA/75

PERI PERI CHICKEN PITTA/76

WEEKDAY MEALS

02

PEA & MINT RIGATONI

I love how vibrant and fresh this pasta dish is. All too often, pasta sauces can be overly rich. However, the pea and mint sauce here is the complete opposite, yet still packed full of flavour. This is especially good when topped with the salty and golden toasted breadcrumbs.

SERVES 4

1 litre (4⅓ cups) boiling water, mixed with 1 chicken stock cube
455g (1lb) frozen peas (preferably petits pois)
400g (14oz) dried rigatoni pasta
Small bunch of mint, leaves only
125g (4½oz) ricotta
Squeeze of lemon juice
Large knob of butter (about 2 tbsp)

To serve (optional)
Toasted breadcrumbs
Grated Parmesan

1 Pour the stock into a saucepan, bring to the boil, then tip in the frozen peas. Bring to a simmer, cook for a few minutes until softened, then drain.

2 Meanwhile, bring a large pan of salted water to the boil, add the pasta and cook for about 10 minutes until al dente (check the packet instructions). Set aside about 230ml (1 cup) of the starchy pasta water, then drain the pasta.

3 Tip the cooked peas into a blender and add the mint, ricotta, lemon juice and a splash of the reserved pasta water. Add sea salt and freshly ground black pepper to taste, then blitz on high until completely smooth. If the sauce is too thick, continue to add more of the reserved pasta water until you reach the desired consistency (the amount needed will vary depending on the type of peas you have used). Add the knob of butter and blitz on high again until emulsified

4 Tip the pasta back into the pan with the pea and mint sauce. Mix well and serve in wide bowls with some crunchy toasted breadcrumbs and a grating of Parmesan, if you like.

ROASTED CHERRY TOMATO CAVATAPPI

This is a wonderful recipe to have up your sleeve. With a mixture of sweet and sour flavours from the tomatoes, lemon and garlic, it is a delicious and fuss-free weeknight meal. The key to a silky smooth tomato sauce is to make sure that the butter is cold when you add it to the blender.

SERVES 4

500g (1lb 2oz) cherry tomatoes
1 red onion, quartered
Grated zest of 1 lemon
2 tbsp olive oil, plus 1 tsp
1 small bulb of garlic
400g (14oz) dried cavatappi pasta
Large knob of cold butter (about 2 tbsp)
Grated Parmesan, to serve

1   Preheat the oven to 200°C (400°F) Gas Mark 6.

2   Place the tomatoes, onion, lemon zest and the 2 tablespoons of olive oil in a roasting tray, season with sea salt and mix it all together.

3   Cut the top off the bulb of garlic (not the root end), rub with the teaspoon of olive oil then wrap tightly in foil. Place the garlic in the corner of the roasting tray.

4   Cook in the oven for about 30 minutes, until the tomatoes are slightly charred and blistered, and the garlic has softened.

5   Cook the pasta in a large pan of salted, boiling water for about 10 minutes, or until al dente. Drain, saving some of the cooking water, and place it back in the pan.

6   Tip the tomatoes and onion into a blender. Remove the bulb of garlic from the foil and squeeze the cloves into the blender as well. Add 2 tablespoons of the reserved pasta cooking water and blitz on high until smooth. Add the knob of cold butter and continue to blitz until it has melted and emulsified. The sauce should now be thick and glossy. Test it for seasoning and add sea salt and freshly ground black pepper to taste.

7   Tip the tomato sauce into the pan of cooked pasta, mix it all together and serve with a good grating of Parmesan on top.

TARRAGON CHICKEN

My favourite thing about this dish is the crispy chicken skin you get at the end. Always make sure to do the last step under the grill, so you can achieve a golden, crisp finish. This dish goes nicely with some steamed greens and buttery mashed potatoes (see page 71).

SERVES 2

1 tbsp olive oil
2 whole chicken legs
1 medium onion, finely chopped
3 garlic cloves, finely sliced
Small bunch of tarragon, leaves finely chopped
300g (10½oz) portobello mushrooms, finely sliced
200ml (scant 1 cup) chicken stock
3 tbsp crème fraîche

1   Add the olive oil to a shallow flameproof casserole over a medium heat. Add the chicken legs and fry skin side down for 7–8 minutes, until golden brown. Remove from the pan and set aside.

2   Add the onion to the same pan and fry over a medium heat for 5–6 minutes until soft and starting to caramelize.

3   Add the garlic and tarragon and cook for a couple of minutes, making sure not to burn the garlic.

4   Add the mushrooms, season with sea salt and freshly ground black pepper, and cook for 8–10 minutes until they have released some of their moisture and are slightly browned.

5   Add the stock, turn the heat to medium-high and bring it up to a simmer. Add the chicken, skin side up, and cover with a lid.

6   Cook for 15–20 minutes over a low heat, keeping the sauce at a gentle bubble, until the chicken is completely cooked through.

7   Preheat the grill (broiler) to high, remove the lid from the pan and place under the grill for 6–7 minutes to crisp up the chicken skin.

8   Remove the chicken from the pan, stir in the crème fraîche and serve.

HERBY BREADCRUMB SALMON TRAYBAKE

Who doesn't love a traybake?! I find that salmon can be overwhelmingly rich, but with the acidity of the tomatoes and the fresh, herby breadcrumb topping, you get a lovely balance of flavours and textures here.

SERVES 4

2 x 400g (14oz) cans of butterbeans, drained and rinsed (490g/1lb 1oz total drained weight)
750g (1lb 10oz) cherry tomatoes
1 tbsp olive oil
3 tsp dried oregano
4 x 125g (½oz) salmon fillets
4 tsp Dijon mustard
Squeeze of lemon juice

For the topping
40g (½ cup) fresh breadcrumbs
30g (¼ cup) pistachios
1 tbsp roughly chopped dill
1 tbsp roughly chopped flat-leaf parsley
Grated zest of 1 lemon
1 tbsp olive oil

1   Preheat the oven to 180°C (350°F) Gas Mark 4.

2   Spread the butterbeans out in a roasting tray with the cherry tomatoes, olive oil and oregano, and season with sea salt and freshly ground black pepper. Roast in the oven for 10 minutes.

3   Meanwhile, add all the topping ingredients to a blender and blitz together for a few minutes until combined.

4   Pat the salmon fillets dry, place skin side down and brush 1 teaspoon of mustard over the top of each. Equally divide the breadcrumb topping between the tops of each salmon fillet, pressing down so that it sticks in place.

5   Remove the tomato tray from the oven, lay the salmon fillets on top, then roast for another 15 minutes until the salmon is cooked through and flaky, the tomatoes are slightly charred and the butterbeans are softened.

6   Mix the tomatoes and butterbeans together, mashing a few butterbeans and tomatoes together to make a thick, chunky sauce.

7   Serve the butterbean-tomato sauce on plates, then lay the salmon fillets over the top and dress with a squeeze of lemon juice.

CREAMY SAUSAGE & MUSHROOM PASTA

This definitely hits the spot when you are craving something indulgent, but easy to cook, after a long day. This dish can vary, depending on the sausages you choose, so feel free to pick a different variety if you want to mix things up. Personally, I love making this with a spiced Italian sausage.

SERVES 4

8 Cumberland sausages (feel free to change this up if you'd prefer a more spicy or herby sausage)
1 red onion, finely diced
1 tbsp olive oil
3 garlic cloves, thinly sliced
4 sprigs of thyme, leaves only
300g (10½oz) portobello mushrooms, sliced
400g (14oz) dried conchiglie pasta
130ml (generous ½ cup) double (heavy) cream
20g (scant ¼ cup) grated Parmesan
Bunch of flat-leaf parsley, leaves roughly chopped, to garnish

1 Cut a slit down the side of each sausage, peel off the skin and crumble the sausage meat into a cold sauté pan. Turn the heat to medium and cook for 10 minutes until browned and caramelized, breaking up the sausage meat into smaller chunks with a spatula as it cooks. Remove the meat and set aside.

2 Add the onion to the pan, with the olive oil, if needed. Cook for 10 minutes until starting to caramelize, then add the garlic and thyme and cook for a few more minutes.

3 Add the mushrooms to the pan of onion, season with sea salt and freshly ground black pepper, cover with a lid and leave to cook for another 10 minutes over a medium heat.

4 Bring a large pan of salted water to the boil and cook the pasta until al dente (check the packet instructions), about 10 minutes.

5 Meanwhile, add the cream, Parmesan and sausage meat to the pan with the mushrooms, and cook over a medium-high heat for 5–10 minutes until the sauce has thickened.

6 Once the pasta is cooked, drain it, reserving 100ml (scant ½ cup) of the cooking water, then tip it into the pan with the sausage. Add the reserved pasta water, mix together and cook for a few more minutes until the pasta is cooked through to your liking.

7 Check for seasoning, then serve in bowls with a sprinkling of parsley to garnish.

TAMARIND & COCONUT CAULIFLOWER STEAKS

Who said vegetarian food needs to be boring? The tamarind and coconut sauce is a dream, especially when garnished with the pomegranate seeds and toasted almond flakes. The key to a good cauliflower steak, regardless of the sauce, is to get a good sear on both sides of the steak to give it that necessary depth of flavour. Serve this with creamy mashed potatoes (see page 71) or garlicky stir-fried greens.

SERVES 3–4

1 head of cauliflower
1½ tbsp tamarind paste
2 tsp smoked paprika
1 tbsp olive oil
3 garlic cloves, minced
½ tbsp honey
1 x 400ml (14fl oz) can of coconut milk
Dash of oil for frying (such as peanut or vegetable)
Knob of butter (about 2 tbsp)
4 tbsp plain yogurt
2 tbsp pomegranate seeds
Zest of 1 lime
1 tbsp almond flakes, toasted

1 Preheat the oven to 200°C (400°F) Gas Mark 6.

2 Remove the leaves from the cauliflower then cut it into 3 x 2.5cm (1-inch) steaks. Save the remaining florets to add to the roasting tray later. Season the cauliflower with a sprinkle of sea salt and some freshly ground black pepper.

3 In a roasting tray, mix the tamarind paste, smoked paprika, olive oil, garlic, honey and coconut milk together, and season with salt and pepper.

4 Heat the frying oil in a large frying pan over a medium-high heat. Lay the cauliflower steaks in the pan and sear for 4–5 minutes on the first side until browned, then flip, add the butter to the pan and baste the steaks with the foamy butter. After another 4–5 minutes, when the second side has browned, remove the steaks from the pan and place into the prepared roasting tray.

5 Spoon some of the sauce over the cauliflower then roast in the oven for 10–15 minutes until the sauce has thickened and the cauliflower has cooked through.

6 Serve the steaks with the delicious coconut sauce drizzled over, then top with some yogurt, pomegranate seeds, lime zest, toasted almond flakes and a pinch of flaky sea salt.

PORK CHOPS WITH CHIMICHURRI

These go really well with Mini Rosemary Roast Potatoes (see page 186). The most important step to this recipe is rendering the pork fat. If you make sure to do this, every bite will be melt-in-your-mouth.

SERVES 4

4 pork chops, 2.5cm (1inch) thick
4 tbsp peanut or vegetable oil
4 knobs of butter (about 8 tbsp)
4 small bunches of tarragon

For the chimichurri
2 small bunches of flat-leaf parsley, leaves finely chopped
1 red chilli, finely chopped
1 large garlic clove, grated
6 tbsp olive oil
1 tbsp red wine vinegar
½ tbsp dried oregano

1 Score the fat on the pork chops to prevent them from curling up in the pan. Season both sides with sea salt and freshly ground black pepper.

2 Heat half the oil in a frying pan over a medium-high heat. Lay 2 pork chops in the pan fat side down, turn the heat down to medium and cook for a few minutes to render the fat. Lay the chops flat side down and cook for 2 minutes, then flip over.

3 Add half the butter and tarragon to the pan and cook for 3 minutes on the second side, basting throughout.

4 Remove the chops from the pan and leave to rest while you cook the others. When they are all cooked, prepare the chimichurri.

5 To make the chimichurri, mix all the ingredients in a bowl and season with sea salt to taste.

6 Drizzle the chimichurri over the chops and serve alongside some delicious roast potatoes.

SPICY TORTILLA

Spanish tortillas will always be an ultimate comfort food. The Italian influence from the 'nduja in this dish brings it to a whole new level. Of course, nothing beats a classic, but this is my personal favourite way of making a tortilla. Serve it alongside a lightly dressed leafy green salad for the ideal weeknight meal.

SERVES 4–6

600g (1lb 5oz) Charlotte potatoes (or any other waxy variety)
4 tbsp olive oil
1 large leek, diced
3 small garlic cloves, minced
Large sprig of thyme
3 tbsp 'nduja paste
5 large eggs, beaten

1 Slice the potatoes into discs, roughly 3mm (⅛inch) thick and place in a 23cm (9inch) deep frying pan over a medium-high heat. Add 3 tablespoons of the olive oil, season with sea salt and fry for 15–20 minutes until golden. Remove to a large bowl and set aside.

2 Add the leek to the pan with the remaining tablespoon of olive oil, some sea salt, the garlic and thyme. Sauté for 5 minutes over a medium heat until softened. Add the 'nduja paste, cook for 5 more minutes, then tip everything into the bowl with the potatoes. Mix together and spread out in an even layer in the pan.

3 Add the eggs and some freshly ground black pepper to the pan and cook over a medium heat for 10 minutes until golden on the bottom and most of the top is set (a slightly runny top is ok).

4 Place a plate on top of the pan, flip the tortilla upside down onto the plate, then slide it back into the pan so the second side can cook for 10 minutes until crispy.

5 Slide out onto a plate or chopping board, cut into segments and serve.

MUSHROOM RISOTTO

One of the tastiest risottos I've ever eaten was on the small Venetian island of Burano. The stand-out element was its creaminess. This is what I've tried to replicate here. The key is using hot stock and stirring continuously. The combination of thyme, mushrooms, parsley and toasted breadcrumbs, makes for a very tasty risotto. Any leftovers can be used for the arnacini recipe on page 161.

SERVES 4–6

40g (1½oz) dried porcini mushrooms, cut into bite-sized pieces
200ml (scant 1 cup) just-boiled water
1 tbsp olive oil
60g (4 tbsp) butter
300g (10½oz) wild mushrooms, cut into small pieces (if you can't find wild, use a 50:50 mixture of chestnut and portobello mushrooms)
2 shallots, finely diced
4 sprigs of thyme, leaves only
3 garlic cloves, grated
300g (1½ cups) arborio rice (don't rinse it)
50ml (scant ¼ cup) white wine
1 litre (4⅓ cups) hot chicken stock
50g (½ cup) grated Parmesan
Bunch of flat-leaf parsley, leaves finely chopped, to garnish

For the truffle breadcrumbs
40g (¾ cup) panko breadcrumbs
2 sprigs of thyme, leaves finely chopped
2 tbsp truffle oil, plus extra to garnish

1   Add the porcini mushrooms to a heatproof bowl and cover with the just-boiled water. Leave to soak until ready to use.

2   Add the olive oil and a third of the butter to a pan and place over a medium heat. Add the fresh mushrooms and cook for 15 minutes until they have started to brown. Remove from the pan and set aside.

3   To the same pan, add the shallots and sauté for 5 minutes until softened and translucent. Add the thyme and garlic, season with sea salt and freshly ground black pepper, and cook for a few more minutes. Turn the heat to high and add the rice. Stir it into the shallots and toast for 2 minutes. Pour in the wine to deglaze and cook for a few minutes until most of the wine has evaporated.

4   Preheat the oven to 200°C (400°F) Gas Mark 6.

5   Strain the porcini, keeping the soaking water, and set aside with the other mushrooms. Mix the soaking water with the hot chicken stock.

6   Over a medium heat, gradually add the stock to the pan, one ladle at a time, stirring continuously. Repeat until all the stock has been used. Continue to cook for a few minutes until the rice is done to your liking.

7   Meanwhile, mix the panko breadcrumbs, thyme and truffle oil together in a bowl. Spread out on a baking sheet and toast in the oven for 5 minutes until golden.

8   Remove the risotto from the heat and stir in the mushrooms, saving a few for garnishing later. Sprinkle in the Parmesan and add the remaining butter. Give this a good mix to incorporate and emulsify the risotto.

9   Check for seasoning, then serve in shallow bowls, topped with a sprinkle of parsley, a drizzle of truffle oil and some truffle breadcrumbs.

PRAWN SAGANAKI

This is my take on the classic Greek dish. The better the quality of the tinned tomatoes, the tastier the dish will be. Feel free to use whole prawns to get even more flavour into the sauce (you will need roughly double the weight for a similar serving size).

SERVES 4

3 tbsp olive oil, plus extra to drizzle
1 onion, diced
3 garlic cloves, sliced
1 tbsp dried oregano
1 tsp dried chilli flakes
75ml (⅓ cup) white wine
1 x 400g (14oz) can of chopped
   tomatoes
Pinch of caster (superfine) sugar
300g (10½oz) raw king prawns
   (shrimp), shells removed
   (prepared weight)
150g (1⅓ cups) crumbled feta
Small bunch of flat-leaf parsley,
   leaves finely chopped
Squeeze of lemon juice
Crusty bread or pittas, to serve

1 Preheat the oven to 200°C (400°F) Gas Mark 6.

2 Heat the oil in a frying pan over a medium-high heat. Add the onion and fry for 5 minutes until softened. Stir in the garlic, oregano and chilli flakes, and season with sea salt and freshly ground black pepper. Cook for 5 more minutes.

3 Turn the heat to high, then deglaze the pan with the white wine. Simmer until most of the liquid has evaporated, then add the tomatoes and sugar and cook for 15 minutes, until the sauce has thickened considerably.

4 Line a baking tray with a layer of foil, followed by a larger layer of baking parchment. Mix the prawns into the tomato sauce and pour into the middle of the baking parchment. Sprinkle the feta over the top with a drizzle of olive oil. Wrap the parchment into a tight parcel and either tie the top with string, or wrap the parcel in a layer of foil to seal. Bake in the oven for 25–30 minutes.

5 Remove from the oven and untie the parcel – there will be lots of steam so be careful. Place in the middle of the table, sprinkle with parsley and a squeeze of lemon juice, and serve with some crusty bread or warm pittas.

SPICED CAULIFLOWER SOUP

The mix of spices and textures in this soup, when combined with the garnishes, make it the perfect comfort food for a cold and rainy day.

SERVES 3–4

1 head of cauliflower
1 tbsp olive oil
1 small bulb of garlic
1 leek, diced
Knob of butter (about 2 tbsp)
2 tsp curry powder
900ml (4 cups) chicken stock
Toasted sourdough croutons, to
    serve (optional)

For the chilli-garlic oil
4 garlic cloves, minced
4 tsp dried chilli flakes
2 bunches of flat-leaf parsley,
    leaves finely chopped
4 tbsp olive oil

1   Preheat the oven to 170°C (340°F) Gas Mark 3½.

2   Cut the cauliflower into florets and place in a large roasting tray. Drizzle with the olive oil and season with some sea salt and freshly ground black pepper. Cut the garlic bulb in half around its circumference, wrap tightly in foil and place in the corner of the same roasting tray. Place the tray in the oven and roast for 20 minutes until the cauliflower has some colour. Remove the cauliflower from the tray and place the garlic back in the oven for 10 minutes to finish cooking.

3   In a large saucepan over a medium heat, fry the leek in the butter for 5 minutes until softened. Add the curry powder and cook for a few more minutes.

4   Once cooked, place the roasted cauliflower in the saucepan and squeeze the garlic cloves from the bulb into the pan as well. Add the chicken stock and bring to a simmer. Cover with a lid and cook over a medium heat for 10 minutes.

5   Meanwhile, add the minced garlic, chilli flakes and parsley to a heatproof bowl. Heat the oil in a saucepan until very hot, then pour this over the garlic mixture. It will sizzle vigorously for a bit. Mix and leave to cool before serving.

6   Remove the soup from the heat and blend using a hand-held blender. Check the seasoning to taste.

7   Serve in soup bowls with a drizzle of the chilli oil on top, and some toasted sourdough croutons.

GNOCCHI CARBONARA

A good carbonara is one of the undisputed go-to pasta dishes for many people. Most commonly, spaghetti is used. However, when paired with fresh gnocchi the starchiness of the potato thickens the sauce, leaving you with the most velvety, unctuous carbonara you can imagine. Purists will say that using guanciale is key here, but this can be hard to find. Fatty pancetta will work just as well in my opinion, and can be a cheaper alternative.

SERVES 2

3 egg yolks
40g (1½oz) pecorino, grated, plus
   extra to serve
80g (¼oz) guanciale (use pancetta
   if you can't find guanciale), cut
   into small pieces
500g (1lb 2oz) gnocchi

1   Put the egg yolks, pecorino and plenty of freshly ground black pepper in a bowl. Mix thoroughly until a paste forms.

2   Place the guanciale in a cold frying pan. Turn the heat to medium-high and cook until golden and crispy, about 10 minutes. Take off the heat and set aside a third of the guanciale to use as a topping.

3   Bring a large pan of salted water to the boil and tip in the gnocchi. Cook for a few minutes until they float to the top and are soft. Drain, reserving 150ml (⅔ cup) of the starchy water.

4   Tip the gnocchi into the pan of guanciale and add the cheese and yolk mixture. With the pan offf the heat, gradually add 100ml (scant ½ cup) of the reserved starchy cooking water, stirring continuously so you don't overcook the egg. Keep doing this until you have a silky-smooth sauce. You might need more, or less, water depending on how starchy the gnocchi is.

5   Serve in bowls topped with extra pecorino, black pepper and the reserved crispy guanciale.

CRAB LINGUINE

This dish comes with many memories for me. Going on family holidays to the coast when I was younger, crab linguine would be a family favourite that we would make together. Fresh crab is the key here. As with any dish that only has a few ingredients, especially when meat and fish are involved, the better the quality and freshness of that particular ingredient, the tastier the dish will turn out. If you can't access fresh crab easily, save this recipe to make as a treat for an occasion when you can. It is worth it.

SERVES 2

200g (7oz) dried linguine
Knob of butter (about 2 tbsp)
2 garlic cloves, minced
1 red chilli, finely chopped
100g (3½oz) fresh brown and white crab meat (fresh is essential here), kept separate
2 tbsp finely chopped flat-leaf parsley, plus extra to garnish
Grated zest and juice of ½ lemon

1   Bring a pot of salted water to the boil, add the linguine and cook until al dente (a couple of minutes less than the timings on the back of the packet), about 10 minutes.

2   Meanwhile, melt the butter in a pan over a medium heat and cook for 3 minutes until it starts to brown (this will add a nice nuttiness to the dish).

3   Turn the heat to down to low, add the garlic and chilli and toast for 1 minute. Add the brown crab meat to the pan, mix thoroughly and set aside.

4   Once cooked, drain the linguine, reserving 80ml (⅓ cup) of the cooking water.

5   Place the brown crab meat pan back over a low heat. Add the linguine, white crab meat and reserved pasta water. Mix thoroughly until emulsified, then add the parsley, lemon zest and juice, and season with sea salt and freshly ground black pepper.

6   Toss together to combine and serve in wide bowls with a sprinkling of parsley to finish.

BUTTERNUT SQUASH ORZO

The most important part of this recipe is to use a squash (or gourde alternative) that is in season; that way it will be full of flavour. Roasting caramelizes the squash, which gives a lovely richness to the dish and, once the squash has broken down and is mixed into the orzo, it creates a beautifully thick and creamy sauce.

SERVES 4

550g (1lb 4oz) butternut squash
   (about half a large squash),
   peeled and cut into 1cm (½inch)
   slices
1 tbsp olive oil, plus extra to drizzle
1 tbsp cumin seeds
1 litre (4⅓ cups) chicken stock
250g (9oz) orzo
Knob of butter (about 2 tbsp)
3 tbsp plain yogurt
Small bunch of flat-leaf parsley,
   leaves finely chopped

1   Preheat the oven to 220°C (425°F) Gas Mark 7.

2   Mix the butternut squash slices with the olive oil and cumin seeds, and season with sea salt and freshly ground black pepper.

3   Line a baking tray with baking parchment and spread the squash out in a single layer. Roast in the oven for 25 minutes until they have some nice colour on them.

4   While the squash is cooking, add the stock to a pan and bring to the boil. Season with sea salt, add the orzo and give it a mix. Turn the heat down to medium-low so it reaches a gentle simmer. Cover with a lid, cook for 10 minutes, then take off the heat and leave to steam for another 10 minutes.

5   Once the squash has cooked, remove it from the oven and tip into a bowl. Mash with a fork until you have a lumpy purée, then stir this into the orzo (which should have soaked up lots of the liquid and grown significantly in size), along with the butter.

6   Stir in the yogurt (don't mix it all in, having streaks of yogurt is nice in this dish) and parsley, then serve in wide bowls, with a drizzle of oil and a few cracks of black pepper to garnish.

CRISPY CHICKPEA DAL

Dal is one of the great comfort foods. Sitting down to a big bowl of dal is always incredibly warming and fulfilling. The addition of crispy chickpeas gives this dish a distinct nutty flavour and textural difference.

SERVES 4–6

250g (9oz) dried red lentils
200g (7oz) cherry tomatoes
1 × 400g can of chickpeas
    (240g/9oz drained weight)
2 tbsp olive oil
2 tsp ground coriander
2 tsp garam masala
2 white onions, diced
2 tbsp ghee (or use 1 tbsp butter
    and 1 tbsp olive oil combined)
4 garlic cloves, minced
3 dried chillies
1 × 2.5cm (1inch) knob of fresh root
    ginger, grated
1 tbsp ground cumin
1 litre (4⅓ cups) chicken stock
Large bunch of coriander (cilantro),
    leaves roughly chopped

1   Preheat the oven to 220°C (425°F) Gas Mark 7.

2   Rinse the lentils in a sieve (strainer) then place in a bowl of water to soak for 30 minutes.

3   Place the cherry tomatoes and chickpeas on a roasting tray and cover with 1 tablespoon of the olive oil, the ground coriander and garam masala, and season with sea salt and freshly ground black pepper. Mix together, then roast in the oven for 20 minutes until the tomatoes are slightly charred and blistered.

4   Remove from the oven, scoop out the tomatoes, then add the remaining tablespoon of oil to the chickpeas, place the tray back in the oven and roast for another 10 minutes for the chickpeas to crisp up.

5   Meanwhile, add the onions and ghee to a saucepan and cook for 5 minutes over a medium-high heat until starting to brown.

6   Add the garlic, dried chillies, ginger, cumin and roasted cherry tomatoes, and season with sea salt and freshly ground black pepper. Mix it all together, crushing up the tomatoes, then turn the heat down to medium and cook for another 5 minutes, stirring often.

7   Once the chickpeas have crisped up, take them out of the oven, lift them from the tray and place them on kitchen paper to dry.

8   Drain the lentils then tip them into the onion pan. Pour over the chicken stock, bring to a simmer, cover with a lid and cook for 40 minutes over a low heat, stirring every 10 minutes. After 40 minutes, open the lid halfway and leave to cook for another 15–20 minutes until the dal has thickened.

9   Once ready, stir through the chopped coriander and sprinkle over the crispy chickpeas to serve.

ITALIAN-STYLE MEATBALLS

The thick tomato sauce is the best part about this dish.

SERVES 4–6

2 tbsp olive oil
1 onion, finely diced
2 tbsp water
75g (scant 1 cup) fresh
 breadcrumbs
250g (9oz) minced (ground) beef
 (20% fat)
250g (9oz) minced (ground) pork
 (20% fat)
2 bunches of thyme, leaves finely
 chopped (1–2 tbsp)
2 small sprigs of rosemary, needles
 finely chopped (1–2 tbsp)
3 gratings of nutmeg
1 large egg
Small bunch of chives, finely
 chopped, to serve

For the sauce
2 shallots, sliced
2 garlic cloves, grated
Bunch of thyme, leaves only (about
 1 tbsp)
2 x 400g (14oz) cans of chopped
 tomatoes
Splash of red wine (optional)
300ml (1⅓ cups) water

For the mash
6 large white potatoes (such as
 Maris Piper) (950g/2lb 2oz)
150ml (⅔ cup) whole milk, warmed
Knob of salted butter (about 2 tbsp)
15g (about 1 tbsp) grated
 Parmesan, plus extra to serve

Note: Traditionally Italian meatballs
are around 60g (¼oz), but I prefer
small ones. If you make these for a
meatball sub, go for the larger size.

1 Heat 1 tablespoon of the olive oil in a pan over a medium heat. Add the onion and water and cook for 10 minutes until softened. Set aside to cool.

2 Add the breadcrumbs to a large bowl, with the beef and pork mince, thyme, rosemary, nutmeg, egg and cooled onions, season with sea salt and freshly ground black pepper and mix well until combined.

3 Divide the mixture into 18 meatballs, each 40g (1½oz) – see Note, if you prefer larger meatballs. Place them in the fridge to chill for an hour – this step helps prevent them from falling apart when searing.

4 Heat the remaining tablespoon of olive oil in a sauté pan over a medium-high heat. Fry the meatballs for 7 minutes until browned on all sides. Remove from the pan and set aside.

5 To the same pan, add the shallots, garlic and thyme, season with a pinch of sea salt and cook for a few minutes over a medium heat. Add the tomatoes, splash of red wine, if using, and water, and season with freshly ground black pepper. Bring to a simmer over a medium-high heat and cook for 15 minutes until the tomatoes have broken down.

6 Add the seared meatballs, cover and cook over a medium heat for 15–20 minutes until the meatballs are cooked through and the sauce has thickened.

7 Meanwhile, prepare the mashed potatoes. Peel the potatoes and cut into even chunks, then place in a pan of cold, salted water. Bring to the boil and cook for 10–15 minutes or until soft (when a cutlery knife goes through easily). Drain in a colander and then, in batches, use a metal spoon to squash the potatoes through a fine mesh sieve (strainer). This may take an extra 5 minutes or so, but is worth it for the silky-smooth result. Add the warmed milk, butter and Parmesan and mix together until smooth. Test for seasoning and adjust if needed.

8 Serve the meatballs on top of a bed of smooth mash, with plenty of sauce drizzled over the top. Top with a grating of Parmesan and a sprinkle of finely chopped chives.

CHICKEN ADOBO

Chicken adobo is an incredibly popular dish from the Philippines. The mix of sweet, sour and salty flavours is what makes this so recognisable and tasty. I first came across it from a Filipino friend of mine and since then have developed my own take on the dish. The uniform-sized pieces allow the adobo to cook quickly, making it perfect for a weeknight meal.

SERVES 4

6 skinless and boneless chicken thighs, cut into bite-sized pieces
4 large potatoes, peeled and cut into bite-sized pieces (450g/1lb)
1 onion, diced
Small knob of fresh root ginger (10g/¼oz), peeled and julienned
4 garlic cloves, grated
165ml (¾ cup) rice wine vinegar
200ml (scant 1 cup) light soy sauce
3 bay leaves
3 tbsp honey
1 tbsp olive oil
3 spring onions (scallions), finely sliced, to garnish

1   Mix all the ingredients except the olive oil and spring onions in a bowl. Season with salt and lots of black pepper, cover and leave to marinate in the fridge for 1 hour, if you have time.

2   Heat a sauté pan over a medium-high heat and add the olive oil. Remove the chicken from the marinade and fry for a 6–7 minutes to give it some colour. Once slightly browned, set aside.

3   Add the rest of the marinated ingredients and the marinade to the pan, cover with a lid and simmer for 15 minutes. Return the chicken to the pan, turn down the heat to medium-low and cook for a final 10 minutes, until everything has cooked through and the sauce has thickened.

4   Serve over steamed rice and garnish with the spring onions.

PANEER BUTTER MASALA

This curry goes really well with some fresh garlic naan and is one of my favourite ways to eat paneer. You could use another type of protein, such as chicken, with the same sauce.

SERVES 4–6

2 blocks of paneer (450g/1lb in total), cut into cubes about 2.5cm (1inch)
100g (scant ½ cup) plain yogurt
Small knob of fresh root ginger (15g/½oz), grated
4 garlic cloves, grated
2 tsp ground coriander
2 tsp ground cumin
Juice of ½ lemon
Crispy fried onions, to serve

For the sauce
115g (1 cup) cashew nuts
250ml (generous 1 cup) just-boiled water
3 tbsp ghee (or butter)
2 onions, diced
1 large cinnamon stick
10 cardamom pods
3 tsp ground cumin
3 tsp ground coriander
3 tsp chilli powder
3 tsp kasoori methi or fenugreek seeds
Pinch of turmeric
4 large garlic cloves, grated
Small knob of fresh root ginger (15g/½oz), grated
2 tbsp tomato paste
200ml (scant 1 cup) double (heavy) cream, plus extra to garnish
Large knob of butter (about 2 tbsp)

1   Mix the paneer in a bowl with the yogurt, spices and lemon juice and leave to marinate overnight, or for at least 3 hours.

2   For the sauce, soak the cashews in the just-boiled water and leave to sit until ready to use.

3   Melt the ghee in a pan over a medium-high heat. Add the onions, cinnamon and cardamom, season with sea salt then cook for 15 minutes until starting to caramelize.

4   Turn the grill (broiler) to high. Assemble the paneer on some skewers, then place them under the grill for about 10 minutes, turning every 2½ minutes until you get a nice char on all sides. Remove from the grill and take off the skewers. Set aside.

5   Add the cumin, coriander, chilli powder, kasoori methi, turmeric, garlic, ginger and tomato paste to the onion pan. Turn the heat to medum, mix everything together and cook for 2–3 minutes.

6   Drain the cashews (saving the water) then add them to the pan with the cream and cook for a few more minutes.

7   Discard the cinnamon stick, then tip it all into a blender and blitz on high until completely smooth. With the blender still running, stream in the water used to soak the cashew nuts.

8   Tip the sauce back into the pan, add the cooked paneer and the knob of butter, mix together and heat through for 5–10 minutes. If needed, add a splash more water, depending on how thick you like the sauce. Ideally it should be a little thicker than the consistency of double cream. Check the seasoning and adjust to taste.

9   Top with some crispy fried onions and a drizzle of cream, then serve with steamed basmati rice or naan.

PERI PERI CHICKEN PITTA

Peri peri chicken is hugely popular in restaurants around the world. This recipe shows you how to make it at home. The tanginess of the lemon zest in the sauce paired with the charring on the outside of the chicken is what makes this stand out to me. The sauce can be stored in an airtight container in the fridge for 1–2 weeks, or frozen, and can be used in many other dishes as well.

SERVES 2

4 chicken thigh fillets, skin on
5 tbsp peri peri sauce (see below)
Olive oil, for brushing
2 tbsp plain yogurt
2–4 pittas, warmed
Shredded lettuce
Pickled red onions (see page 107)
Bunch of coriander (cilantro),
   roughly chopped

For the peri peri sauce
½ red onion, roughly chopped
225g (8oz) roasted red peppers
   (jarred are perfect)
1 scotch bonnet chilli, deseeded, or
   3 regular red chillies (for a milder
   sauce)
4 garlic cloves
Grated zest of 1 lemon
Juice of 1½ lemons
1 tbsp smoked paprika
1 tbsp dried oregano
2 small sprigs of rosemary, needles
   only
2 tbsp red wine vinegar
4 tbsp olive oil

1 Place the chicken in a bowl with 3 tablespoons of the peri peri sauce and season with sea salt. Mix together until incorporated.

2 Heat a griddle pan (cast-iron works best) over a medium-high heat. When up to temperature, place the chicken in the pan, skin side down.

3 Cook for 5 minutes on each side, then turn up the heat to high and cook for a further 3 minutes on each side to get a good charring all over – this is where all the flavour is. Throughout the cooking process, use the remaining peri peri from the bowl mixed with a splash of olive oil, and brush it over the chicken to keep it juicy. Once cooked, remove the chicken from the heat and rest for 5 minutes.

4 Mix the yogurt with the remaining 2 tablespoons of peri peri sauce and a pinch of sea salt to taste.

5 Slice the rested chicken into strips, then place in the warm pittas with the yogurt and peri peri sauce, lettuce, pickled onions and coriander.

PERI PERI SAUCE

1 Place all the ingredients in a blender and blitz to a smooth purée.

2 Tip into a pan and cook over a low heat for 15 minutes, stirring continuously, then remove from the heat and leave to cool slightly.

3 Tip back into the blender, turn it to high and slowly stream in the olive oil until the sauce is smooth and emulsified.

LEMONGRASS & PEARL BARLEY CHICKEN THIGHS/80

PORK RIBS WITH CUCUMBER SLAW/83

MUSHROOM RAGU/84

FRESH PASTA DOUGH/87

RIBEYE RAGU/88

LAMB SHANK PHO/91

AUBERGINE TAGINE/92

CHILLI CON CARNE/94

HERBY CHIPOTLE CASSOULET/95

BIRRIA BOWLS/97

LAMB KLEFTIKO/98

QUICK PREP, SLOW COOK

03

LEMONGRASS & PEARL BARLEY CHICKEN THIGHS

This dish is one of my favourites in the book. The flavours are heavily inspired by Southeast Asian cuisine and work really well with the pearl barley and crispy chicken thighs. The wonderful thing about pearl barley is that it has the ability to soak up and absorb all the amazing flavours and juices. This dish would go well alongside some sautéed greens with a squeeze of lemon on top.

SERVES 3–4

6 skin-on, bone-in chicken thighs, excess loose skin removed
1 onion, sliced
1 large lemongrass stalk, bashed with a rolling pin
Grated zest of 1 lime
Juice of 2 limes
4 garlic cloves, sliced
1 large red chilli, finely chopped
3 makrut lime leaves
1 x 400ml (14fl oz) can of coconut milk
450ml (2 cups) water
200g (7oz) pearl barley, rinsed
Bunch of coriander (cilantro), leaves roughly chopped

1 Preheat the oven to 180°C (350°F) Gas Mark 4.

2 Add the chicken thighs skin side down to a flameproof casserole, wide enough to hold all the chicken pieces in one layer. Place over a medium-high heat and cook for 5 minutes to render the fat. Remove the chicken from the pan and set aside.

3 To the same pan, add the onion and lemongrass and fry over a medium heat for 5 minutes in the chicken fat. Add the lime zest and juice, garlic, chilli, lime leaves, and a few pinches each of sea salt and freshly ground black pepper. Cook for 5 more minutes then add the coconut milk and water. Bring to a simmer, stir in the pearl barley, then place the chicken thighs on top, skin side up.

4 Place in the oven, uncovered, and cook for 1 hour until the chicken skin is golden and crisp. Remove the dish from the oven, lift out the chicken and discard the lemongrass and lime leaves. Stir the coriander through the pearl barley.

5 Serve the pearl barley with the crispy chicken thighs on top.

PORK RIBS WITH CUCUMBER SLAW

Slow-cooked pork ribs, grilled with a sticky glaze . . . you just can't beat it! Making this for lots of people is a fail-safe way to impress. A little trick is to crumble a stock cube into the marinade – this is a quick and easy way to add depth and a rich, umami flavour.

**SERVES 3–4 AS A MAIN OR
4–6 AS PART OF A SPREAD**

1.2kg (2lb 10oz) individual pork ribs
   (each 85–150g/3–5½oz)
120ml (8 tbsp) water

For the marinade
3 tbsp olive oil
5 tbsp red wine vinegar
6 tbsp honey
2 tbsp smoked paprika
2 tsp garlic powder
1 chicken or vegetable stock cube,
   crumbled

For the cucumber slaw
2 cucumbers, halved, deseeded
   and julienned
2 tbsp rice wine vinegar
1 garlic clove, crushed
1 tsp dried chilli flakes

1   Mix the marinade ingredients together in a bowl, seasoning with sea salt and freshly ground black pepper. Pour the marinade over the ribs and leave to marinate in the fridge overnight, or at least a few hours.

2   When ready to cook, preheat the oven to 160°C (325°F) Gas Mark 3.

3   Place the ribs in a baking tray, pour the water into the base of the tray and tightly cover the tray with foil. Cook in the oven for 2 hours, until tender.

4   Meanwhile, mix the slaw ingredients together in a bowl, season with sea salt, then cover and refrigerate until ready to serve.

5   Remove the ribs from the oven and lay them on a new tray, pouring the tray juices into a small saucepan. Place the saucepan of juice over a high heat and reduce until thickened.

6   Preheat the grill (broiler) to high then brush the ribs with some of the reduced juices. Cook under a grill for 4–5 minutes until slightly charred on top then remove them from the oven.

7   Brush the ribs one more time with the reduced juices, then serve with the cucumber slaw.

MUSHROOM RAGÙ

I absolutely love cooking with king oyster mushrooms. Shredding them with a fork gives you wonderfully long strands that work incredibly well in this dish. It is a great alterntive to a meat-based ragù.

SERVES 4

325g (11½oz) king oyster
  mushrooms
4 tbsp olive oil
20g (¾oz) dried porcini
  mushrooms
100ml (scant ½ cup) just-boiled
  water
2 onions, diced
2 celery stalks, finely chopped
3 garlic cloves, sliced
Bunch of thyme, leaves only
  (1 tbsp)
3 tsp chipotle paste
3 tsp tomato paste
1 tbsp cornflour (cornstarch)
1 litre (4⅓ cups) vegetable stock
400g (14oz) dried pappardelle
  pasta or fresh (see page 87)

1 Preheat the oven to 180°C (350°F) Gas Mark 4.

2 Shred the king oyster mushrooms using a fork, scraping down the stem until it resembles that of pulled meat, and you have lots of mushroom strands. Place on a roasting tray, cover in 1 tablespoon of the olive oil and a pinch of flaky sea salt and mix to coat evenly. Roast in the oven for 30 minutes until golden, mixing the mushrooms around after 15 minutes to prevent them from sticking to the tray.

3 Put the dried porcini mushrooms in a heatproof bowl, pour over the just-boiled water and set aside to soak.

4 Heat the remaining 3 tablespoons of olive oil in a sauté pan over a medium heat. Add the onions and celery with a pinch of sea salt and cook for 15 minutes until they are starting to caramelize. Add the garlic and thyme and cook for 3 more minutes.

5 Add the roasted mushrooms, chipotle paste and tomato paste to the pan. Cook for 3 minutes to bring out the flavours of the pastes, then add the cornflour, season with freshly ground black pepper and mix together.

6 Gradually mix in the stock, constantly stirring so no lumps form. Once combined, add the porcini and their soaking water, cover with a lid, reduce the heat to low and gently cook for 1½ hours, stirring every 30 minutes. If you see the ragù is getting too dry, add a splash of water.

7 Remove from the heat and set aside while you cook the pasta.

8 Bring a large pan of salted water to the boil and cook the pappardelle according to the packet instructions, if using dried, or for 3–4 minutes if using fresh. Drain, place in a pan and mix with the ragù before serving.

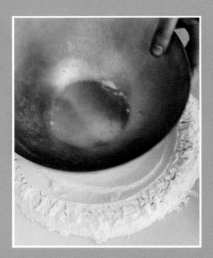

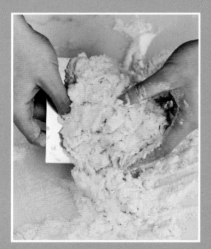
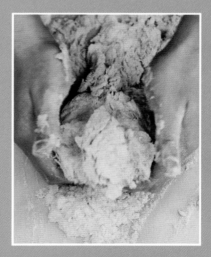
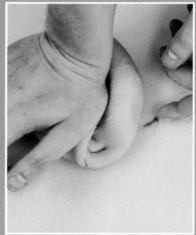
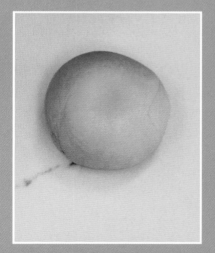

MADE FROM SCRATCH
FRESH PASTA DOUGH

You could go with a basic dough recipe but the below combination is my favourite and worth the extra effort sourcing the ingredients. After all, making fresh pasta isn't something you do all the time, so when you do it, why not make it the best you can.

SERVES 4

150g (5½oz) tipo 00 flour
150g (5½oz) fine semolina
1½ tsp fine sea salt
3 medium eggs (160g/5½oz total
    weight without shell), at room
    temperature

Note: Roll the dough out for different shapes (setting 6 for fettucine; 7 for filled), laminate it and roll out on each setting multiple times.

1   Mix the flour, semolina and salt in a bowl. Tip out onto a clean work surface and make a well in the centre, using the bottom of the bowl.

2   Crack the eggs into the well and beat together with a fork. Gently start to incorporate the flour into the egg, until all of it has been combined and you have a shaggy dough (lumpy, yet well-mixed).

3   Set the fork aside and use your hands to bring the dough together, collecting up all the loose bits. Start to knead the dough by pushing down and away slightly, rotating 45 degrees then pushing down and away. Note that this is a lot stiffer than a regular bread dough so won't be as soft and stretchy when you knead.

4   Keep kneading for about 10 minutes until the dough is smooth and the flour and egg are nicely incorporated with each other.

5   Wrap in clingfilm (plastic wrap) and rest for 2 hours at room temperature before rolling (see page 140).

RIBEYE RAGÙ

Feel free to use beef short ribs instead of ribeye steaks for a more luxurious meal. Equally, if you're looking for a cheaper alternative, use a shoulder cut. This would also be a perfect filling for the tortellini on page 140.

SERVES 4

1 tbsp neutral-flavoured oil, such as vegetable or peanut
700g (1lb 9oz) ribeye steaks, cut in half
2 onions, finely diced
2 carrots, finely diced
2 celery stalks, finely diced
3 garlic cloves, sliced
80ml (⅓ cup) wine (any colour)
3 tbsp tomato paste
1 litre (4⅓ cups) beef stock
Small bunch of thyme
3 bay leaves
1 x 400g (14oz) can of chopped tomatoes
400g (14oz) dried pappardelle pasta (or make fresh pasta dough, see page 87)

Beef: This is searing, not stewing, so make sure the heat is high and the meat gets good colour. There is nothing worse than 'browning' meat for it to go grey and stew in its own juices. This is an important step for flavour and tenderness.

Onions: Browning is flavour! In fact, a little charring will add an amazing depth. In Mexican cuisine, charring is used a lot to bring incredible smokiness to dishes. In Italian cuisine, which is the inspiration for this ragù, charring isn't usually a thing, but it's a game-changer here.

1   Preheat the oven to 160°C (325°F) Gas Mark 3.

2   Heat the oil in a flameproof casserole over a high heat. Season the meat with sea salt and freshly ground black pepper, then sear in batches (don't overcrowd the pan) for 1–2 minutes on each side until browned (see Note below). Once all the meat has been seared, set it aside, leaving all the juices and oils in the pan.

3   Add the onions, carrots, celery and a pinch of sea salt to the pan and sauté over a medium-high heat until browned, and starting to char (see Note below). Add the garlic and cook for 1 more minute.

4   Turn the heat to high, add the wine and cook for a few minutes until most of the liquid has evaporated.

5   Turn the heat down to medium, add the tomato paste and cook for 3 minutes. Add the beef stock, thyme, bay leaves, chopped tomatoes and seared meat. Bring to a simmer, cover with a lid and cook in the oven for 3½ hours until the meat is falling apart and tender, checking on it halfway through and giving it a stir. If the meat doesn't pull apart easily after cooking, leave it in the oven slightly longer.

6   Bring a large pan of salted water to the boil and cook the pappardelle for about 10 minutes until al dente (check the packet for specific timings), then drain.

7   Remove the ragù from the oven, pull apart the meat, mix it all together and serve with the parpardelle. Save leftovers for the homemade tortellini on page 140, it's a must!

LAMB SHANK PHO

This recipe is my twist on a Vietnamese pho. The most important part, of course, is the broth. Take your time to cook it and you will be rewarded with a delicious, aromatic bowl of goodness. Make sure to mix everything together before tucking in.

SERVES 6

1.5kg (3lb 5oz) lamb shanks
1 tbsp olive oil
600g (1lb 5oz) flat rice noodles (bahn pho)
2 bunches of mint, leaves only
Large bunch of coriander (cilantro), leaves only
Large bunch of Thai basil, leaves only
2 red chillies, finely sliced
Handful of beansprouts (roughly 60g/2¼oz per portion)
2 limes, cut into wedges, to serve

For the broth
8 star anise
2 small cinnamon sticks
4 cardamom pods
1½ tbsp coriander seeds
7 black peppercorns
2 white onions, peeled and halved
1.5 litres (6½ cups) chicken stock
1.5 litres (6½ cups) water
Large knob of ginger (50g/1¾oz), skin on, sliced
2 tsp sugar
3 spring onions (scallions), finely sliced
1½ tbsp fish sauce

1   Place the star anise, cinnamon, cardamom, coriander seeds, peppercorns and onions on a baking tray, then place under the grill (broiler) on high for a minute until the spices have toasted (be careful not to burn them). Remove the spices and set aside, then put the onion back under the grill for another 5 minutes until blackened on top.

2   Preheat the oven to 130°C (260°F) Gas Mark ½.

3   Season the lamb shanks with some sea salt and freshly ground black pepper. Heat the oil in a large casserole over a medium-high heat. Add the lamb shanks and sear for a few minutes on each side until browned.

4   Turn the heat down, pour in the stock and water, then add the toasted spices, charred onions, ginger and sugar. Bring to a simmer, cover with a lid and cook in the oven for 6–7 hours, checking every 2 hours, giving it a stir and adding more water if it is looking dry. Once cooked, the lamb should be tender and falling off the bone.

5   Remove the meat from the broth and set aside. Strain the rest of the broth through some cheesecloth, discard the vegetables and spices, then pour the broth back into the pan. Stir in the spring onions, add the fish sauce and adjust to taste – if it needs more salt, use more fish sauce. The flavour should be mild, warming and comforting. Pull the lamb meat off the bone.

6   Soak the rice noodles in just-boiled water until softened, about 10–15 minutes, then rinse under cold water to prevent them clumping together.

7   Serve the noodles in 4 large bowls, then pour over the warm broth. Top with some shredded lamb, and garnish each bowl with a handful of mint, coriander and Thai basil leaves, finely sliced red chillies, a handful of beansprouts and a lime wedge.

AUBERGINE TAGINE

I love a good tagine so here's my twist on that classic dish. The star here is rose harissa. If you can't get hold of this, however, regular harissa will work too. As with all tagines, give it time to cook down; the flavours will intensify and you'll be left with a rich, sweet and sour stew.

SERVES 3–4

2 aubergines (eggplants), cut into large 2cm (¾-inch) chunks (490g/1lb 1oz in total)
3 tbsp olive oil
100g (3½oz) rose harissa paste
150g (1 cup) medjool dates, finely chopped
500ml (2¼ cups) just-boiled water
2 onions, sliced
4 large garlic cloves, sliced
1 x 400g (14oz) can of chopped tomatoes
1 x 400g (14oz) can of chickpeas, drained and rinsed
Handful of flaked (slivered) almonds, toasted in a dry pan for a few minutes until fragrant
Small bunch of flat-leaf parsley, finely chopped
Squeeze of lemon juice
4 warmed flatbreads, to serve

1 Add the aubergines to a bowl with 1 tablespoon of the olive oil and the harissa paste, and season with sea salt and freshly ground black pepper. Mix until evenly coated, then leave to marinate while you prepare the other ingredients.

2 Put the dates in a heatproof bowl, cover in the just-boiled water and leave to soak until needed.

3 Preheat the oven to 160°C (325°F) Gas Mark 3.

4 Add the remaining 2 tablespoons of olive oil to a sauté pan over a medium-high heat. Add the onions and garlic and cook for 10 minutes until softened and translucent, then remove from the pan and set aside. Add the aubergine to the same pan, with another splash of olive oil if needed, turn the heat up to medium-high and fry for 10 minutes until they get some nice colour on them.

5 Add the dates and their soaking water, along with the softened onions and chopped tomatoes to the pan. Mix, cover with a lid and transfer to the oven to cook for 1½ hours, checking after 45 minutes and stirring.

6 After 1½ hours, add the chickpeas and toasted almonds (saving a few to garnish), then place back in the oven to cook for a further 1 hour. Once cooked, the tagine should be thick, rich, sweet and spicy.

7 Plate it up in some bowls, sprinkle with parsley and the reserved toasted almonds. Squeeze over some lemon juice and serve with a warm flatbread on the side.

CHILLI CON CARNE

In my opinion, the only way to make a decent chilli is to pack it full of spices, sear the mince really well and cook it for so long the meat gets incredibly tender and the sauce is thick and rich. There is nothing worse than chewy bits of undercooked mince. The tomato salsa brings a nice freshness. Best served with some steamed basmati rice (see page 200).

SERVES 4

1 tbsp olive oil
500g (1lb 2oz) minced (ground) beef
1 onion, diced
3 garlic cloves, minced
2 tsp ground cumin
2 tsp ground coriander
2 tsp smoked paprika
1 tsp chilli powder
3 tsp chipotle paste
1 green bell pepper, deseeded and diced
1½ tbsp cornflour (cornstarch)
1 x 400g (14oz) can of chopped tomatoes
2 squares of dark chocolate (30g/1oz)
700ml (3 cups) beef stock
1 x 400g (14oz) can of kidney beans, drained and rinsed

For the tomato salsa
300g (10½oz) cherry tomatoes, finely chopped
Large bunch of coriander (cilantro), leaves finely chopped, plus extra to garnish
1 large jalapeño chilli, finely chopped
1 tbsp olive oil

1 Preheat the oven to 140°C (275°F) Gas Mark 1.

2 Add the olive oil to a flameproof casserole and place over a high heat. Season the beef mince with some salt, then sear it in batches until browned. This will take 4–5 minutes. When browned, remove from the pan and set aside.

3 To the same dish, add the onion with a pinch of salt and cook for 10 minutes until softened. Add the garlic, spices, chipotle paste and green pepper, and season with freshly ground black pepper. Cook for 5 minutes, then stir in the cornflour and cook for a few more minutes.

4 Add the tomatoes and chocolate, mix, then add the stock and seared beef. Cover with a lid and cook in the oven for 3 hours, stirring every hour until reduced and tender. Mix through the kidney beans 30 minutes before the end.

5 While the chilli is cooking, prepare the tomato salsa by mixing all the ingredients in a bowl with sea salt and black pepper. Adjust the spice level to taste.

6 Once cooked, remove the chilli from the oven, and serve topped with some tomato salsa and the reserved coriander leaves.

HERBY CHIPOTLE CASSOULET

This well-known French stew is a winner on a cold wintery day. The cut of pork used here makes for a lovely balance of flavours and textures. This is one of those meals that can be prepared in advance and reheated throughout the week for lunches and dinners, without having to compromise on flavour.

SERVES 4

1 tbsp olive oil
300g (10½oz) pork shoulder, cut into 3cm (1¼inch) dice
4 sausages
1 white onion, diced
1 large carrot, finely diced
4 garlic cloves, minced
1 tbsp thyme leaves, finely chopped
1 tbsp tomato paste
80ml (⅓ cup) white wine
2 x 400g (14oz) cans of cannellini beans, drained and rinsed
1.2 litres (5¼ cups) chicken stock
1 bay leaf
150g (5½oz) rainbow chard, roughly chopped

1   Preheat the oven to 160°C (325°F) Gas Mark 3.

2   Add the olive oil to a wide flameproof casserole and place over a high heat. Sear the pork shoulder and sausages for a few minutes until brown on all sides. Remove and set aside.

3   Turn the heat to medium-low, add the onion and carrot to the pan and cook for 5 minutes until softened. Add the garlic, thyme and tomato paste and season with sea salt and freshly ground black pepper. Cook for a few more minutes.

4   Turn the heat up to medium-high, deglaze the pan with the white wine and allow most of it to evaporate. Add the pork shoulder, sausages and cannellini beans, mix together, then pour in the stock. Add the bay leaf, bring to a gentle simmer, then cover with a lid and cook in the oven for 1 hour.

5   Remove the lid and return to the oven to cook for 45 minutes uncovered.

6   Stir in the rainbow chard and cook for a final 30 minutes, still uncovered.

7   Once cooked, the meat should be tender and the cannellini beans should have soaked up and thickened lots of the liquid.

BIRRIA BOWLS

Birria has to be one my favourite Mexican foods. I love it served with crispy tostadas, guacamole and sour cream . . . what's not to love? The meat here is very rich, so you won't need huge portions, especially when served with tostadas (see page 29) and side salads and salsas (see page 180). If you can, try to use the proper dried chillies, which can be found online at a good price.

SERVES 6–8

4 plum tomatoes
1 white onion, peeled and halved
6 garlic cloves, peeled
850g (1lb 14oz) boneless beef shoulder, cut into a few large pieces
2 tbsp olive oil
6 guajillo chillies, deseeded and stalks removed
3 ancho chillies, deseeded and stalks removed
2 árbol chillies (if you want a bit more of a spicy kick), deseeded and stalks removed
1 litre (4⅓ cups) beef stock
1 tbsp ground cumin
1 tbsp dried oregano
2 bay leaves
1 cinnamon stick
1 tbsp red wine vinegar

For the toppings
Sour cream
Guacamole
Lime wedges
Finely sliced red chilli
Coriander (cilantro) leaves
Tostadas (see page 29)

1 Place the tomatoes, onion and garlic on a baking tray and place under the grill (broiler) on high for 5–10 minutes, until charred.

2 Preheat the oven to 160°C (325°F) Gas Mark 3.

3 Season the beef with some sea salt. Heat the olive oil in a casserole over a high heat then sear the beef on all sides for a few minutes until browned.

4 Turn the heat down to medium and add the charred vegetables and remaining ingredients. Bring to the boil, cover with a lid, then cook in the oven for roughly 3 hours until tender and falling apart, giving it a stir every hour and topping up with extra stock if it is looking dry.

5 Once cooked, remove from the oven and lift out the meat. Set aside while you prepare the sauce. Tip everything remaining in the casserole, except the bay leaves and cinnamon stick, into a blender and blitz on high until smooth. Pull apart the meat, then pour over three-quarters of the sauce and mix to combine. Save the extra sauce for people who want more on top of each portion, or to dip tortillas and tacos into.

6 Serve the meat in bowls and top with dollops of sour cream, guacamole, lime wedges, chilli and coriander, and serve with tostadas, side salads and salsas.

LAMB KLEFTIKO

I've spent a lot of time in Greece and lamb kleftiko is one of those dishes that always stands out for me. Wrapping the lamb in layers of parchment and foil before cooking ensure juicy, tender meat every single time. Cooking the potatoes at the bottom of the parcel is one of the best things about this recipe, as they take on all the incredible flavours from the lamb. Choosing a waxy variety of potato is key here, so they hold their shape and don't turn into mush.

SERVES 6–8

2.5kg (5lb 8oz) shoulder of lamb
15 garlic cloves, halved
1.5kg (3lb 5oz) Charlotte potatoes, halved (any waxy potato will do)
40ml (about 3 tbsp) red wine
40ml (about 3 tbsp) water

For the marinade
5 tbsp olive oil
2 tsp ground cinnamon
2 tbsp ground cumin
2 tbsp dried oregano
3 sprigs of rosemary, needles roughly chopped
3 tbsp white wine vinegar

1 Using a sharp knife, pierce 30 holes in the top of the lamb shoulder (to fit the garlic).

2 Mix the marinade ingredients in a bowl, with a few pinches of flaky sea salt and plenty of freshly ground black pepper. Spread the marinade evenly across the lamb and fill all the holes with the halved garlic cloves.

3 Line a roasting tin with a layer of foil and then a layer of baking parchment, leaving enough of each hanging over the sides to wrap around the lamb and seal tightly later on.

4 Place the potatoes in the tin and season with sea salt and freshly ground black pepper. Mix until all the potatoes are evenly coated. Place the lamb on top of the potatoes and pour the red wine and water around the lamb inside the parchment. Wrap the entire shoulder tightly in the parchment and foil layers. If needed, wrap one more time in foil to fully seal as we don't want steam to escape. Place in the fridge to marinate overnight.

5 Preheat the oven to 140°C (275°F) Gas Mark 1 and remove the lamb from the fridge.

6 Cook the lamb in the oven for 4 hours until tender and falling off the bone, then remove, unwrap carefully (it will be incredibly hot with all the built-up steam) and lift the lamb onto a chopping board.

7 Lift out the potatoes and place them in a bowl to serve. Gently tease apart the lamb with some tongs and drizzle over the remaining juices from the tin.

ALL OUT

04

CHICKEN GYROS

If you've been to Greece, I'm sure gyros needs no explanation (actually pronouced *yee-ross*). For those who don't know, it is a Greek-style kebab. This recipe makes it easy to replicate gyros at home, maintaining the flavours you'd find in the classic version. There are a few variations of this kebab, but chicken is my favourite and works incredibly well with the other fillings. Gyros paired with an ice-cold beer on a summer's day — *chef's kiss*!

SERVES 6–8

3 tbsp olive oil
1 tbsp dried oregano
2 tsp smoked paprika
1 tsp ground cumin
Juice of ½ lemon
2 garlic cloves, minced
1 tsp honey
800g (1lb 12oz) skinless chicken thigh fillets
2 red onions, halved

To serve
Pittas (see page 105)
Tzatziki (see page 107)
1 red onion, halved and sliced
2 beef (beefsteak) tomatoes, sliced crossways (place the tomato on its side and cut from the base to the top; this way the seeds won't fall out)
French fries (see page 201)
Dried oregano
Squeeze of lemon juice

1 In a bowl, mix the olive oil, oregano, smoked paprika, cumin, lemon juice, garlic, honey, and sea salt and freshly ground pepper to taste. Add the chicken thighs and mix, then cover and leave to marinate for at least 2 hours, or ideally overnight in the fridge.

2 Preheat the oven to 200°C (400°F) Gas Mark 6.

3 Poke 3 skewers through one of the onion halves, slide to the bottom, then poke the skewers through a chicken thigh. Stack the chicken onto the skewers until it is all used up. Finish by adding the second onion half to the top, to lock the chicken in place.

4 Place the skewered chicken on its side in a large roasting tray, add the remaining 2 onion halves to the base of the tray, then roast in the oven for 30 minutes, turning halfway through. Turn the oven temperature up to 220°C (425°F) Gas Mark 7 and roast for a final 15 minutes to get some browning and char on the outside. The internal temperature of the chicken should be around 75°C (167°F).

5 Once ready, remove the chicken from the oven and rest for 10 minutes before carving the meat off the skewers into thin slices.

6 To serve, take a freshly made pitta and add a generous layer of tzatziki on the bumpy side of the bread. Add a portion of meat, some thinly sliced red onions and tomatoes, and some French fries. Sprinkle with dried oregano, squeeze over some lemon juice, wrap up, and enjoy!

GREEK-STYLE PITTAS

I find it hard to get good-quality Greek pittas where
I live, so the best thing for me is to make them myself.
If you have the time, this can take your gyros to a
whole new level. The pitta dough is very versatile
and can be used in plenty of other recipes as well
– see page 165 for French Onion Flatbreads.

MAKES 8

500ml (2¼ cups) warm water
15g (5 tsp) dried active yeast
15g (3½ tsp) caster (superfine)
  sugar
800g (1lb 12oz) strong white
  bread flour
16g (2½ tsp) fine sea salt
4 tbsp olive oil

Note: Keeping the pittas in a slightly
damp tea towel allows them to
continue steaming and get even
softer.

1 In a jug (pitcher), mix the water, yeast and sugar. Leave to sit for 10
   minutes to bloom the yeast (it's ready when it turns bubbly).

2 In a bowl, mix together the flour and salt. Once the yeast mixture has
   bloomed, tip this into the flour with the olive oil and mix.

3 Knead the dough for 10 minutes until smooth and elastic, then place in a
   lightly oiled bowl, cover and leave to prove for 1–2 hours, until doubled in
   size. This time will depend on the temperature of the room – a very warm
   room can take as little as 1 hour and a colder room can take upwards of 2
   hours.

4 Once risen, knock the air out of the dough and tip out onto a clean work
   surface. Divide into 8 equal portions, gently roll into balls with the palm of
   your hand, then cover with a damp tea (dish) towel and leave to rest for 1
   hour.

5 Once rested, roll each portion out into a circles 1cm (½ -inch) thick and
   dimple one side with your fingers.

6 Heat a nonstick frying pan over a medium-high heat. Once hot, place a
   pitta in the pan and cook for about 1 minute on each side. Once cooked,
   set aside and cover with a slightly damp tea towel until ready to serve
   (see Note).

ADANA KEBAB

This recipe is my take on a Turkish adana kebab — many countries around the world have their own versions of this too. All too often, when people try to make this at home, they end up with a dry, chewy and fairly inedible result. The key to a juicy kebab is to buy lamb mince with 15–20% fat, season it well with salt and to make sure you slowly stream in the cold water while you blend. The water helps lock in the moisture and creates the ideal paste to shape onto the skewers. Serving these with all of the side dishes makes for an incredible feast.

MAKES 4 LARGE SKEWERS

500g (1lb 2oz) minced (ground) lamb (15–20% fat)
1½ tsp fine sea salt
½ tsp garlic powder
Bunch of flat-leaf parsley, leaves chopped
Small bunch of coriander (cilantro), leaves chopped
1 tbsp ground coriander
1 tbsp ground cumin
Grated zest of 1 lemon
Good grating of nutmeg
Oil, for brushing

To serve
Pickled red onions (see opposite)
Silky-smooth hummus (see opposite)
Pittas (see page 105; roll them out thinner)
Pickled green chillies
Lemon wedges
Za'atar, to garnish

1   Add all the ingredients except the oil to a blender, with plenty of freshly ground black pepper, and blend on high for a few minutes until a thick paste is formed.

2   Gradually stream in 1 tablespoon of cold water while the blender is running (this helps keep moisture in the kebabs), until smooth.

3   Divide the kebab mixture equally into 4, then, using a slightly wet hand, shape the mixture onto 4 skewers, pressing it into the skewer so it doesn't slide off when cooking. Place in the fridge until ready to cook.

4   Over a lightly oiled griddle pan or BBQ (grill), grill the skewers for 5–6 minutes on each side until they are slightly charred. Alternatively, you can do this under the grill (broiler) on high. As they cook, brush the skewers with oil every now and again.

5   Once cooked, lay the skewers, pickled red onions, hummus, pittas, pickled chillies, lemon wedges and za'atar out on the table for everyone to help themselves to.

MAKES 1 LARGE JAR

10 black peppercorns
½ tbsp mustard seeds
1 tbsp coriander seeds
220ml (1 cup) water
220ml (1 cup) apple cider vinegar
1½ tsp salt
2 tsp sugar
3 red onions, halved and finely
 sliced

PICKLED RED ONIONS

1 Add all the spices to a dry frying pan and toast for 5 minutes over a medium heat until fragrant.

2 Add the water, vinegar, salt and sugar to a saucepan and place over a medium heat until the salt and sugar have dissolved. Bring to the boil, then remove from the heat.

3 Place the onions in a large sterilized jar, tip in the toasted spices and shake to evenly distribute. Pour over the pickling liquid, seal and leave for at least a few hours before using. Store in the fridge for up to 2–3 weeks.

MAKES 500G (1LB 2OZ)

2 x 400g (14oz) cans of chickpeas,
 drained and rinsed
50g (about 3 tbsp) tahini
Juice of 1 lemon
120ml (8 tbsp) olive oil
2 ice cubes

SILKY-SMOOTH HUMMUS

1 Add all the ingredients except the ice cubes to a blender, with sea salt to taste, then blitz. Gradually incorporate the ice cubes while blitzing, until very smooth. Check for seasoning and adjust to taste. Set aside until ready to use.

MAKES 300G (10½OZ)

½ large cucumber
250g (generous 1 cup) thick
 Greek yogurt
1 garlic clove, minced
1 tbsp olive oil
1 tbsp roughly chopped dill
Juice of ½ lemon

TZATZIKI

1 Cut the cucumber in half lengthways and scrape a teaspoon down the middle to remove the seeds. Grate the cucumber then place in a tea (dish) towel and squeeze out as much excess moisture as you can. Place the cucumber in a colander, sprinkle with some fine sea salt and leave to drain for at least an hour, ideally overnight.

2 In a bowl, mix together the yogurt, garlic, olive oil, dill, lemon juice and cucumber with fine sea salt to taste. Refrigerate for a few hours before eating to let the flavours mellow.

MONKFISH CURRY

While I was in India, I visited Bengal, where they are well known for their amazing variety of fish dishes. This inspired me to create a fish curry once I was back home, using my memories of all the wonderful flavours out there.

SERVES 4

2 tbsp cumin seeds
2 tbsp coriander seeds
½ tbsp mustard seeds
Pinch of ground turmeric
4 tbsp ghee (or butter)
380g (13½oz) monkfish, cut into small chunks (any meaty white fish will do)
2 large onions, diced
6 garlic cloves, minced
1 small green chilli, diced
Large knob of ginger (20g/¾oz), grated
850ml (3¾ cups) water
2 pinches of caster (superfine) sugar
Juice of ½ small lemon
3 makrut lime leaves
80g (generous ⅓ cup) plain yogurt
Bunch of coriander (cilantro), leaves chopped

1 Add the cumin, coriander and mustard seeds with the turmeric to a dry frying pan, and toast over a medium heat for 3 minutes until fragrant, then blitz into a fine powder in a small food processor or hand-held blender, or crush in a pestle and mortar.

2 Add 3 tablespoons of the ghee to a pan over a medium-high heat. Add the monkfish and fry for 4–5 minutes until browned. Remove from the pan and set aside.

3 Turn the heat down to medium and add the onions to the pan with the remaining ghee. Cook for 10 minutes until starting to caramelize, then add the garlic, chilli, ginger and spices, and cook for another 3 minutes.

4 Add the water, sugar, lemon juice and lime leaves, season with sea salt and freshly ground black pepper, cover with a lid and cook for 20 minutes over a medium-low heat, then remove the lid and cook for a further 10 minutes over a medium heat. Once the sauce has reduced a bit, remove the lime leaves and tip the rest into a blender with the yogurt and blitz until smooth.

5 Tip the sauce back into the pan, add the chunks of fish and cook for a final 10 minutes until the fish is cooked through. Test the sauce for seasoning and adjust to taste. If you would like the sauce thicker, continue to cook to reduce it further. If you would like the sauce thinner, add a splash more water.

6 Remove the pan from the heat, stir in the coriander leaves and serve with steamed basmati rice (see page 200).

CHICKEN & SPINACH PIE

A hearty pie is a meal that never fails to please. I like to use chicken thighs as they stay juicier and have a lot more flavour than chicken breast. Shortcrust pastry is a must here – the flaky, buttery pastry on top, with a slightly soggy underside from all the juice is simply unforgettable.

SERVES 4–6

1 tbsp olive oil

800g (1lb 12oz) skinless and boneless chicken thighs, cut into bite-sized pieces

2 leeks, halved lengthways and thinly sliced

3 garlic cloves, grated

1 tbsp white wine vinegar

35g (2½ tbsp) unsalted butter

35g (4½ tbsp) plain (all-purpose) flour

700ml (3 cups) chicken stock

150g (5½oz) frozen spinach

1½ tsp Dijon mustard

Bunch of parsley, leaves finely chopped

50g (scant ¼ cup) double (heavy) cream

1 egg

For the shortcrust pastry

300g (2½ cups) plain (all-purpose) flour, plus extra for dusting

75g (⅓ cup) cold unsalted butter, cubed

75g (⅓ cup) cold lard, cubed

¼ tsp fine sea salt

4 tbsp water

1   Add the oil to a pan and place over a medium-high heat. Add the chicken and cook for a few minutes until slightly browned. Remove from the pan and set aside.

2   Add the leeks and a pinch of sea salt to the pan and cook for 10 minutes until starting to caramelize. Add the garlic, season with freshly ground black pepper and sauté for 5 more minutes. Add the vinegar and cook for a few minutes until most of the liquid has evaporated. Stir in the butter until it has all melted, then stir in the flour.

3   Gradually add the stock, constantly stirring so it doesn't go lumpy. Once all the stock has been added, add the frozen spinach and mustard and cook for 5 minutes. Remove from the heat, stir in the seared chicken, the parsley and cream and leave to cool.

4   While the filling is cooling, make the pastry. Tip the flour into a large bowl and add the cold cubes of butter and lard. Rub the flour, lard and butter together with your fingertips until it has all crumbled and resembles breadcrumbs. Dissolve the salt in the water, then gradually add the water to the dough while mixing with your hands, until you have used up all the water.

5   Use your hands to bring the dough together, then place it on a lightly floured surface, gently shape and press together into a disc. Cover the dough in clingfilm (plastic wrap) and refrigerate for 45 minutes before using (see Note overleaf).

Recipe continued overleaf

Note: You can refrigerate the pastry for longer, but make sure to remove it from the fridge about 20–30 minutes before you start rolling. This will allow the pastry to soften slightly and it is less ilkely to fall apart and crack. On the whole, it will make the rolling out process a lot easier.

6 Preheat the oven to 180°C (350°F) Gas Mark 4.

7 Tip the cooled filling into a pie dish. If there is a gap between the lip of the pie and the filling, use an upside down egg cup in the middle of the pie dish to support the pastry. Remove the pastry from the fridge and unwrap it. Place on a lightly floured work surface then, using a rolling pin, roll the dough out until roughly 5mm (¼ inch) thick. Cut off a strip of the pastry and set aside (to line the dish).

8 To make an eggwash, beat the egg with 1 teaspoon of water. Lightly brush the edges of the pie dish with the eggwash to help the pastry stick. Line the flat edges of the pie dish edges with strips of pastry, then brush the strips again with eggwash. Using a rolling pin to support it, lay the rolled-out pastry on top of the dish. Press the edges down to seal the pastry to the dish and the lined edges. Use a fork to crimp the dough to the edges of the pie dish then trim off any excess using a sharp knife. Cut two slits, like an 11, next to each other in the middle of the pie and brush the top with the eggwash.

9 Cook in the oven for 30–35 minutes until the top is golden brown. Keep an eye on it so it doesn't brown too quickly. Remove from the oven and serve with mashed potatoes and buttery steamed greens.

SAUCE-FILLED FISHCAKES

Homemade fishcakes are always worth the effort. The key to making a good fishcake is to use the milk from poaching the fish when you make the béchamel. This carries across all the lovely, smoky, lemony flavours from the fish and lemon zest. These fishcakes would go well alongside a simply dressed green salad.

MAKES 9

1kg (2lb 4oz) potatoes
320g (11oz) skinless cod fillets, cut into chunks
250g (9oz) skinless smoked haddock, cut into chunks
800ml (3½ cups) whole milk
Zest of 1 lemon
2 bay leaves
8 peppercorns
Bunch of flat-leaf parsley, leaves chopped
4 egg yolks
60g (¼ cup) unsalted butter
60g (½ cup) plain (all-purpose) flour
50g (2oz) mature Cheddar
30g (1oz) Parmesan, grated
2 tsp Dijon mustard
Vegetable oil, for frying

For the coating
100g (scant 1 cup) plain (all-purpose) flour
2 eggs, beaten
250g (5 cups) panko breadcrumbs

1 Preheat the oven to 200°C (400°F) Gas Mark 6.

2 Put the potatoes on a roasting tray and prick them a few times with a knife. Bake them in the oven for 1 hour and 15 minutes until they are cooked through. Remove them from the oven and leave to cool.

3 Meanwhile, place the fish in a large saucepan with the milk, lemon zest, bay leaves and peppercorns. Heat until just before the milk is boiling, then remove from the heat and cover with a lid. Leave the fish to poach for 30 minutes in the cooling milk.

4 Remove the fish from the milk and discard the bay leaves and peppercorns. Shake off any excess liquid and set the fish aside to cool. Reserve the milk for the mornay sauce.

5 Combine the parsley and egg yolks in a large bowl, then season with sea salt and freshly ground black pepper. Scoop out the cooled potatoes from their skins and add to the bowl. Give the potato a mash with the back of a fork, then add in the fish, breaking it up into flakes with your hands, and mix everything together until well combined.

6 Divide into 9 balls (about 125g/4½oz each) and set aside in the fridge to chill until ready to use.

7 To make the mornay sauce filling, place the butter in a saucepan over a medium heat. When it has melted, add the flour and whisk until combined. Gradually add the poaching milk into the saucepan, whisking all the time, until incorporated. Cook the sauce for a few minutes to remove any floury taste.

Recipe continued overleaf

SAUCE-FILLED FISHCAKES (CONTINUED)

Note: If you don't have an ice cube tray, you can tip the sauce into a container and place it in the freezer until set, but not completely frozen. Then, using a spoon, scoop out small balls of the sauce and wrap the fishcake mixture around that.

8 Remove the sauce from the heat and stir in the Cheddar cheese, Parmesan and mustard. Check the seasoning and adjust if necessary. Pour the sauce into ice cube trays and place in the freezer for a few hours until solidified, ideally frozen (see Note). This step can be done far in advance.

9 To make the fishcakes, remove the fish from the fridge and flatten each ball into a disc. Place a frozen cube of sauce in the centre of each disc, then wrap the fish mixture around the filling until fully enclosed. Shape into balls again and flatten the top slightly to give it that classic fishcake shape.

10 Half fill a heavy-based pan with vegetable oil and heat to 175°C (347°F). Preheat the oven to 180°C (350°F) Gas Mark 4 and place a raised rack in a roasting tin.

11 Place the flour, beaten eggs and breadcrumbs in three separate bowls. Dip each fishcake in the flour and coat it fully. Shake off any excess then dip it into the beaten egg, then finally into the breadcrumbs. Pat the breadcrumbs into the fishcake.

12 Gently place the fishcakes into the hot vegetable oil, cooking three at a time. Fry for 6 minutes until golden and crisp, then remove from the oil using a slotted spoon and place on the prepared tray and into the oven for 10 minutes. Repeat with the remaining fishcakes.

BACON MAC & CHEESE

I find that baking mac and cheese can often lead to overcooked pasta and a dry sauce, so I make mine slightly differently to avoid those two things. Grilling the pasta at the end of cooking instead of baking, gives you that delicious, golden melted cheese on top, while maintaining the gooey sauce underneath.

SERVES 3–4

250g (9oz) bacon lardons
300g (10½oz) dried macaroni
50g (2oz) Cheddar, grated, for the topping

For the mornay sauce
25g (about 2 tbsp) unsalted butter
25g (about 3 tbsp) plain (all-purpose) flour
400ml (1¾ cups) whole milk
Freshly grated nutmeg
125g (4½oz) Cheddar, grated
50g (2oz) Gruyère, grated

1. Add the bacon lardons to a cold frying pan, place over a medium-high and cook for 15 minutes until golden and crispy, and the fat has rendered.

2. Cook the macaroni in a large pan of salted, boiling water, for 2 minutes less than the stated cooking time on the back of the packet. Drain, saving a splash of the starchy cooking water, then tip the macaroni back into the pan with the reserved water.

3. While the macaroni is cooking, make the mornay sauce. Melt the butter in a saucepan over a medium heat. Add the flour, mix it into the butter and cook this roux for a few minutes.

4. Slowly pour the milk into the roux, whisking continuously.

5. Once all the milk has been incorporated, add some freshly ground black pepper and a few gratings of nutmeg, turn up the heat to medium-high and bring to a bubble. Keep stirring and simmering the sauce for 5 minutes until thickened, then remove the pan from the heat, add the cheeses and stir together until melted.

6. Tip the mornay sauce and bacon into the pot of macaroni and mix until incorporated.

7. Turn the grill (broiler) to medium-high. Tip the mac & cheese into an ovenproof serving dish, top with the grated cheese and place under the grill for 5–10 minutes until golden brown on top.

8. Serve right away while hot, oozy and delicious.

MAC & GREENS

A delicious green alternative to the bacon mac and cheese recipe on page 118. When blitzed, the broccoli creates a delicious, earthy, sweet sauce that goes well with the sharp cheese. One thing to note, the crispy kale and breadcrumbs added at the end are a *must*!

SERVES 4–5

300g (10½oz) broccoli, cut into pieces
100g (3½oz) kale, chopped into bite-sized pieces
1 tbsp olive oil
350g (12oz) dried macaroni
1 quantity of freshly made mornay sauce (see page 118)
50g (2oz) Cheddar, grated
Sprinkling of toasted breadcrumbs

1 Preheat the oven to 180°C (350°F) Gas Mark 4.

2 Bring a large pan of water to the boil, add the broccoli and cook for 8–10 minutes until softened, depending on the size. Drain, saving 140ml (scant ⅔ cup) of the cooking water, and place in a blender with the reserved cooking water. Blitz on high until it forms a smooth purée.

3 While the broccoli is cooking, put the kale and olive oil in a roasting tray, season with sea salt and toss to combine. Cook in the oven for 5–7 minutes until crisp and brown.

4 Cook the macaroni in a large pan of salted, boiling water, for 2 minutes less than the stated cooking time on the back of the packet (roughly 6 minutes is a good rule of thumb for al dente macaroni). Drain and tip back into the pan.

5 Tip the mornay sauce, the broccoli purée and half of the crispy kale into the pan. Mix thoroughly to combine, and check the seasoning.

6 Turn the grill (broiler) to medium-high. Tip the mac & greens into an ovenproof serving dish, top with the grated cheese and place under the grill for 5–10 minutes until golden brown on top.

7 Serve right away while hot, then top with the reserved crispy kale and toasted breadcrumbs.

FISH TACOS

This recipe takes inspiration from both Mexican and Indian cuisine. The combination of crispy battered fish, commonly seen in baja tacos, with the yogurt-based green chutney, makes for an incredibly refreshing and unique mouthful.

SERVES 4

550g (1lb 4oz) skinless haddock (any white fish will work)

For the marinade and sauce
60g (2¼oz) coriander (cilantro), stalks and leaves
Grated zest and juice of 2 limes
2 green chillies
4 garlic cloves, peeled
4 tbsp olive oil
8 tbsp thick Greek yogurt

For the batter
80g (¾ cup) cornflour (cornstarch)
240g (2 cups) plain (all-purpose) flour
2 medium eggs
380ml (1⅔ cups) cold sparkling water
Vegetable oil, for deep-frying

To serve
Corn tortillas (see page 29)
Sprigs of coriander (cilantro)
Lime wedges

1 To make the marinade, place the coriander, lime zest and juice, chillies, garlic and olive oil in a blender, and season with sea salt. Blitz together until it forms a paste.

2 Cut the haddock into bite-sized chunks, place in a bowl with half the marinade, mix then leave to marinate in the fridge for 1 hour.

3 Mix the remaining marinade with the yogurt and set aside.

4 Remove the fish from the fridge and bring to room temperature while you prepare the batter.

5 In a large bowl, mix the cornflour and plain flour together. Add the eggs and sparkling water and whisk it all together. Don't overmix; some small lumps are fine.

6 Third-fill a heavy-based saucepan with vegetable oil and heat to 180°C (356°F).

7 In batches, add the fish to the batter and evenly coat each piece. Lift the fish out of the batter and slowly place it away from you into the hot oil. Fry for 4–5 minutes until cooked through and crispy. Lift the fish out of the oil using a slotted spoon, place on a wire rack and sprinkle with sea salt. Allow the oil to come back up to temperature before frying each batch. While finishing off the remaining pieces of fish, the already-cooked fish can be kept on the wire rack in a low-temperature oven to stay warm and crisp.

8 Serve the fish on some warm corn tortillas with a drizzle of the spicy yogurt, some coriander leaves and a squeeze of lime juice.

MUSHROOM TACOS WITH PARSNIP CRISPS

Tacos don't always need to be filled with meat. This mushroom alternative works as a stand-out vegetarian option. The smokiness from the chipotle paste, the umami from the mushrooms and the sweetness and crunch from the parsnip crisps make this taco one to remember.

SERVES 6

600g (1lb 5oz) portobello
  mushrooms
240g (8½oz) shiitake mushrooms
2 tbsp olive oil

For the marinade
5 tsp chipotle paste
2 tbsp olive oil
2 tsp sugar
6 garlic cloves, grated

For the parsnip crisps
Vegetable oil, for shallow-frying
2 parsnips, peeled then pared into
  thin strips using a vegetable
  peeler

To serve
Corn tortillas (see page 29)
Sour cream (optional)
Finely chopped flat-leaf parsley
  leaves (optional)
Squeeze of lime juice (optional)

1   Slice all the mushrooms into strips, mix with the marinade ingredients in a bowl and season with salt and freshly ground black pepper to taste. Cover and leave to marinate for a few hours.

2   Heat the olive oil in a frying pan over a medium-high heat, add the mushrooms and their marinade and fry for 10 minutes until nicely browned, cooked through, and the sauce has reduced and thickened.

3   While the mushrooms are cooking, quarter fill a heavy-based pan with vegetable oil and place over a medium-high heat. Fry the parsnip strips in the oil for 5 minutes until golden brown and crispy. Remove them from the oil, place on kitchen paper and season with flaky sea salt.

4   Serve the mushrooms on warm corn tortillas, topped with some of the parsnip crisps and sour cream, a sprinkling of parsley and a squeeze of lime juice.

STEAK TACOS WITH WALNUT SALSA

My favourite part of this taco is the walnut salsa. It is a toned-down version of a Mexican salsa macha (see page 195) and it works perfectly with the tamarind-marinated, medium-rare steak.

SERVES 4

2 tsp tamarind paste
2 tsp sriracha
2 x 250g (9oz) sirloin steaks, 2.5cm (1 inch) thick
2 tsp peanut oil

For the walnut salsa
5 tbsp neutral-flavoured oil, such as peanut or vegetable
30g (¼ cup) walnuts
6 tsp white sesame seeds
2 tsp dried chilli flakes
10 garlic cloves, minced (about 30g/1oz)
2 tsp honey

To serve
Corn tortillas (see page 29)
Sprigs of coriander (cilantro)
Lime wedges

1 Mix the tamarind paste and sriracha in a bowl and season with sea salt and freshly ground black pepper. Add the steaks, mix and then leave to marinate overnight in the fridge, or a few hours at least. Remove from the fridge and bring to room temperature before cooking.

2 Heat the peanut oil in a frying pan over a high heat. Lay the steaks in the pan, turn the heat down to medium and cook for 2–3 minutes on each side to get a nice sear and medium-rare inside. Remove the steaks from the pan and leave to rest for 5 minutes before slicing.

3 While the steaks are resting, make the walnut salsa. Add all the salsa ingredients except the honey to the same pan the steaks cooked in. Cook over a medium heat for 5–10 minutes until the sesame and garlic have started to turn golden brown.

4 Remove from the heat, tip into a blender with the honey and pulse. You want there to be some texture to it still, so don't overdo the blending. Season with sea salt to taste.

5 Slice up the steaks and serve on warm corn tortillas, with some of the walnut salsa drizzled over the top, fresh coriander leaves and a squeeze of lime juice.

SMASH BURGER

If I had to choose between a thick, gourmet-style burger or a smash burger, the smash burger would always win. These incredibly thin patties, smashed to the surface of the pan, turn out wonderfully browned and caramelized. Always smash the patty straight away so you don't lose any juices from the meat (which is what happens if you wait and cook it a bit). Season the oil in the pan with salt prior to cooking to help prevent the patty from sticking.

MAKES 5 DOUBLE-PATTY BURGERS

500g (1lb 2oz) good-quality minced (ground) beef (20–30% fat)
Sprig of rosemary, needles finely chopped
5 Japanese milk buns (see page 131) or brioche burger buns
½ tbsp high smoke point oil, such as peanut or vegetable

For the chipotle mayonnaise
4 tbsp mayonnaise
1 tsp wholegrain mustard
1 tsp runny honey
3 tsp chipotle paste (may vary depending on how strong your paste is)

For the toppings
10 slices of Applewood smoked cheese
1 head of lettuce, halved lengthways then thinly sliced
1 large beef tomato, thinly sliced and seasoned with sea salt

1 Mix the beef mince and rosemary with sea salt and freshly ground black pepper to taste in a bowl – don't overmix or it will make the burgers tough. Roll the mixture into 10 balls each 50g (1¾oz). Set aside to chill in the fridge until ready to cook.

2 Mix together the chipotle mayonnaise ingredients, seasoning with sea salt and black pepper.

3 Prepare the toppings so they are ready for building the burgers later.

4 Cut the burger buns in half and lightly toast them in a dry pan over a medium heat until golden and crisp.

5 Heat a frying pan (ideally cast-iron or stainless steel) over a high heat. Once hot, add the oil. Sprinkle the pan with some salt to help prevent sticking, then place the beef patties in the pan (in batches, depending on the size of your pan) and immediately press down on top of the meat with the back of a flat spatula or potato masher covered with foil, squishing them as thin as you can, to ideally 5mm (¼ inch) thick.

6 Fry for a couple of minutes until browned on one side, then flip over and lay a slice of cheese on top of each. Add a small splash of water to the frying pan, about 2 tablespoons, being careful with the spitting oil, and cover with a lid to melt the cheese. After a few minutes, remove the patties from the pan.

7 Spread some chipotle mayonnaise on the bases of the burger buns, top with some shredded lettuce, sliced tomato, 2 cheese-topped patties and more chipotle mayonnaise. Close the burger with the other half of the bun and enjoy.

JAPANESE MILK BREAD BURGER BUNS

These are soft, chewy and full of flavour. The yudane is an important step in getting that ideal chew factor.

MAKES 6

1 egg
1 tsp water
10g (3½ tsp) sesame seeds
20g (1½ tbsp) butter, melted

For the yudane
100g (3½oz) strong white bread flour
60ml (4 tbsp) just-boiled water

For the dough
175ml (¾ cup) whole milk
40g (3 tbsp) caster (superfine) sugar
7g (2¼ tsp) dried active yeast
250g (9oz) strong white bread flour
5g (1 tsp) fine sea salt
40g (2½ tbsp) unsalted butter, cubed, at room temperature

Note: The windowpane test is when you take a small portion of dough and gently pull it apart using your hands, lifting it to the light. If you can see light through the dough, without it tearing, then enough gluten development has happened. If this doesn't work, continue to knead and test again.

1 Start by making the yudane as this will need to chill in the fridge before using. Mix the flour with the just-boiled water in a bowl and bring it together until sticky and elastic. Wrap in clingfilm (plastic wrap) and place in the fridge for a few hours, until chilled.

2 For the dough, warm the milk in a pan until lukewarm, then tip into a measuring jug (pitcher) with the sugar and yeast. Mix and set aside for 10 minutes to bloom the yeast (it will appear bubbly).

3 In a bowl, mix the flour with the salt. Tear up the yudane and add to your flour along with the bloomed yeast milk, and bring together with your hands. Knead for a few minutes until all of the flour is hydrated. If you have a stand mixer with a dough hook, this may be helpful.

4 Gradually incorporate the cubes of butter while continuously kneading. Once incorporated, continue to knead for 8–12 minutes until smooth and elastic. Use the windowpane test to tell when it is done (see Note).

5 Place the dough in a lightly oiled bowl, cover with clingfilm and leave in a warm area to double in size, about 2 hours. Timings may vary depending on how warm the room is. Once doubled in size, knock the air out and divide it into 6 equal portions.

6 Press each portion into a circle, then fold the outsides into the middle, to create a ball. Turn the ball upside down and roll with the palm of your hand on a lightly floured surface to create tension and shape. Once you have an even ball, place on lightly oiled baking parchment on a baking tray, leaving space between each one. Cover with lightly oiled clingfilm and leave to rise until increased by another half in size, about 1–1½ hours.

7 Preheat the oven to 190°C (375°F) Gas Mark 5.

8 Beat the egg with the water to make an eggwash. Once the buns have risen, remove the clingfilm and brush each one with the eggwash. Sprinkle each bun with sesame seeds, then bake in the oven for 17–18 minutes until browned and cooked through. If you notice the buns browning too much, simply lay a sheet of baking parchment loosely over the top.

9 Remove the buns from the oven, place on a wire rack, brush with some melted butter and leave to cool fully before eating.

CHICKEN FAJITAS

Chicken fajitas will always be seen as a Tex-Mex classic. Most fajita recipes don't do Mexcian cuisine justice, though, so I wanted to bring a stronger Mexican influence to my recipe. Charring the vegetables prior to frying them, a common technique in Mexican cooking, imparts a wonderful smokiness to the dish that takes it to a whole new level.

SERVES 4

2 bell peppers (any colour), deseeded and cut into thin strips
2 tbsp olive oil
2 small onions, sliced
4 garlic cloves, sliced
3 medium tomatoes, deseeded and finely chopped
500g (1lb 2oz) skinless, boneless chicken thighs, cut into strips 1cm (½ inch) wide

For the spice mix
2 tsp garlic powder
2 tsp onion powder
2 tsp cayenne pepper
3 tsp smoked paprika
3 tsp dried thyme
1 tsp sea salt
1 tbsp brown sugar

To serve
4 flour tortillas, warmed in a griddle pan
Sour cream
Guacamole
Jalapeño chillies
A few sprigs of coriander (cilantro)
Lime wedges

1 To make the spice mix, combine everything together in a bowl. Measure out 3 tablespoons and set aside; store the remainder in an airtight jar for future use.

2 Preheat the grill (broiler) to high then spread the peppers out on a baking tray, skin side up, and grill for 4–5 minutes until the skin has blistered and charred. Remove and set aside.

3 Heat 1 tablespoon of the olive oil in a frying pan over a medium heat. Add the onions and fry for 10 minutes until starting to caramelize. Add the garlic and the 3 tablespoons of spice mix, mix together and cook for 5 more minutes.

4 Add the grilled peppers to the pan along with the tomatoes. Cook for 5 minutes over a medium heat then tip everything out into a bowl.

5 In the same pan, heat the remaining tablespoon of olive oil over a medium-high heat and add the chicken. Fry for 8–10 minutes until cooked through and there is some nice browning on the outside. Return the onion-pepper mixture to the pan and season with sea salt and freshly ground black pepper. Mix together and cook for a few more minutes.

6 Serve in warmed tortillas with some soured cream, guacamole, jalapeños, coriander, and lime wedges to squeeze over.

BUTTERFLIED LAMB LEG WITH MANGO SALSA

I love to cook this for friends and family on a warm spring or summer's day. Butterflying the lamb not only speeds up the cooking process, but helps maintain an evenly cooked finish.

SERVES 8–10

2.2kg (5lb) leg of lamb (boned weight), butterflied to a 5cm (2inch) thickness (see below)
Coriander (cilantro), to garnish

For the marinade
150g (5½oz) chipotle paste
8 garlic cloves, minced
3 tbsp olive oil
2 tbsp smoked paprika

For the mango salsa
2 mangos, flesh cut into small cubes
½ red onion, very finely diced
Large bunch of coriander (cilantro), leaves finely chopped
Grated zest of 2 limes
Juice of 1 lime
2 red chillies, finely diced
2 tsp olive oil

1 Mix the mango salsa in a bowl, adding sea salt to taste, and refrigerate until ready to use.

2 Mix the lamb with the marinade ingredients and some sea salt and freshly ground black pepper, cover and leave to marinate for at least 4 hours, or ideally overnight in the fridge.

3 Preheat a BBQ (grill) to high. Alternatively, use an oven grill (broiler) on high (roughly 220°C/425°F).

4 Place the lamb on the grill and cook for about 40–45 minutes, flipping halfway through, until it has a good colour on both sides. The internal temperature should be around 55°C (131°F) for medium-rare.

5 Remove from the heat and leave to rest for 10 minutes before slicing and laying out on a dish. Spoon the mango salsa over the top of the lamb before serving and top with some coriander sprigs.

'NDUJA CHICKEN KYIV

This is one of those dishes that leaves you feeling very satisfied after you've made it and is definitely one that will impress. It certainly puts all supermarket kievs to shame. The key to this recipe is rolling the chicken around the 'nduja paste – it'll help you get a tight bundle that won't leak when it is fried.

SERVES 4

100g (3½oz) baby leaf spinach
2 tbsp water
100g (scant ½ cup) unsalted butter, at room temperature
4 tbsp 'nduja paste
3 garlic cloves, grated
Bunch of flat-leaf parsley, leaves roughly chopped
50g (2oz) Parmesan, grated
4 skinless and boneless chicken breasts
50g (scant ½ cup) plain (all-purpose) flour
3 large eggs, beaten with 3 tbsp cold water
180g (3½ cups) panko breadcrumbs
Vegetable oil, for shallow-frying
Mashed potato (see page 71)

1 Put the spinach and water in a large pan and cook over a high heat until wilted. Drain well and leave to cool for 5–10 minutes, then squeeze out any excess moisture.

2 Add the butter, 'nduja, garlic, parsley, wilted spinach and Parmesan to a food processor and blitz to a smooth paste.

3 Place the chicken breasts between two large sheets of baking parchment (work with one or two at a time). Using a rolling pin, bash the chicken out to a 1cm (½-inch) thickness.

4 Spread a quarter of the 'nduja mixture onto the centre of each flattened chicken breast, leaving a wide border. Fold the sides inwards and roll the rest up tightly into a log shape to enclose the filling. Place on a plate and chill in the fridge for 30 minutes.

5 Prepare the coating by adding the flour, beaten eggs and breadcrumbs to three separate bowls. Mix the flour with a pinch of fine sea salt.

6 Once chilled, one at a time roll the chicken in the flour, then the egg, followed by the breadcrumbs. Dip back into the egg, then the breadcrumbs, to give them a double coating. Place on a plate and chill for another 30 minutes.

7 Preheat the oven to 180°C (350°F) Gas Mark 4.

8 Third-fill a heavy-based pan with vegetable oil and place over a high heat. Remove the chicken from the fridge. Working in batches, fry the chicken in the hot oil for 6–7 minutes, until golden brown, then transfer to a rack over a foil-lined baking tray. Take care here as the chicken can cause the hot oil to spit.

9 Transfer the tray to the oven and bake for 20–25 minutes, or until the chicken is cooked right through.

10 Serve with mashed potato and some greens alongside.

COURGETTE & LEMON TORTELLINI

Homemade tortellini is a lot of fun to make. Courgette and lemon are two ingredients that work really well together, especially when doused in brown butter.

SERVES 4

1 quantity of fresh pasta dough
   (see page 87)
Tipo 00 flour and semolina, for
   dusting
Few knobs of butter (about 4 tbsp)
Chives, breadcrumbs or grated
   Parmesan, to serve

For the filling
2 courgettes (zucchini), grated
250g (9oz) ricotta
Grated zest of 1 lemon

Notes: You should make 35–45 tortellini, depending on the size of the pasta discs and the amount of filling inside. Any leftover tortellini can be frozen for up to a few months.

If you are making lots of tortellini, cook them in batches. Once a batch has been boiled for 4 minutes, plunge the tortellini into ice cold water to stop them cooking further. When all the tortellini have been cooked, reheat them together in the brown butter.

1 To make the filling, add the grated courgette to a nonstick frying pan (nonstick is important as we don't want to add any oil) and cook over a medium heat for 10 minutes, stirring frequently, until most of the moisture has evaporated. During this time the courgette may brown a little – some colour is totally fine and adds to the flavour. Set aside to cool completely.

2 Add the cooled courgette to a blender with the ricotta, lemon zest, and some sea salt and freshly ground black pepper to taste. Blend on high for a few minutes until completely smooth, then test for seasoning and adjust if necessary. Set aside.

3 Roll the dough out with a rolling pin or to setting 6–7 on your pasta machine, about 1–2mm (1/16–1/8 inch) thick. Always keep the dough lightly dusted with flour throughout the rolling out process and beyond, so it doesn't stick to the rolling pin, pasta machine or kitchen surfaces. If the dough feels a little tacky, sprinkle a light dusting of flour on both sides and brush over it with your hand a few times. Cut the rolled-out dough into circles using a 9cm (3½-inch) diameter round cutter, or an upside-down cup.

4 Spoon a small teaspoon of filling (about 8g/⅛oz) into the centre of each circle. It is very easy to think you need more filling than you do, but don't be tempted to overfill them! Lightly wet your finger and rub around the edges of the circle. Fold in half and press the edges together to form a half-moon shape. Make an indent in the filling and fold one corner around to the opposite corner. Press the corners tightly together to seal. (Refer to the photos on the next page for a visual guide to shaping them.) Place the shaped tortellini on a baking sheet dusted with semolina flour.

5 Bring a pot of salted water to the boil. Add the pasta and cook for 4 minutes.

6 Meanwhile, place the butter in a large frying pan over a medium-high heat until it starts to foam. Turn the heat to low and keep cooking until it browns, then remove from the heat.

7 Once the pasta has cooked, lift it out with a slotted spoon and place into the pan of brown butter. Return the pan to the heat until the butter is hot, then toss the pasta in the butter. Serve with a crack of black pepper and a sprinkling of chives, breadcrumbs or Parmesan to top it off.

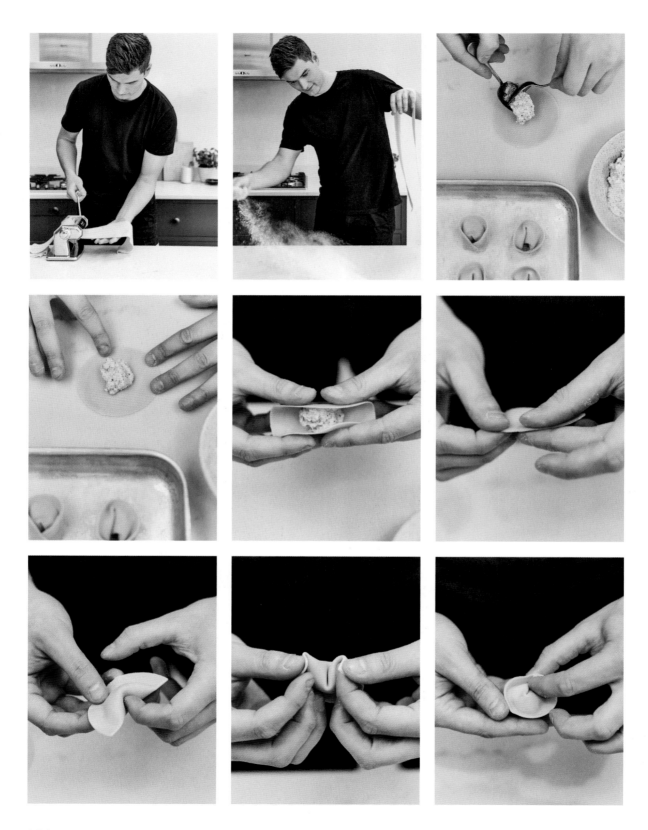

LEMON & HERB CHICKPEA ROAST CHICKEN

This is a great way to jazz up your Sunday roast chicken. The preserved lemons add a freshness and the chickpeas soak up all of the wonderful juices while they cook inside the chicken.

SERVES 4–6

1 large chicken (2kg/4½lb)
1 tbsp olive oil
1 bulb of garlic, cut in half around its circumference

For the chickpea stuffing
4 small preserved lemons, finely chopped
2 tbsp finely chopped flat-leaf parsley
Sprig of rosemary, needles finely chopped
2 tbsp finely chopped dill
1 tbsp olive oil
2 x 400g (14oz) cans of chickpeas, drained and rinsed

For the salsa verde
2 tbsp coriander (cilantro) leaves, finely chopped
2 tbsp flat-leaf parsley leaves, finely chopped
4 tbsp olive oil, plus extra for drizzling
Grated zest and juice of ½ lemon
1 garlic clove, minced

1   Take the chicken out of the fridge to room temperature 30 minutes before cooking and place in a roasting tin. Preheat the oven to 200°C (400°F) Gas Mark 6.

2   In a large bowl, mix together the stuffing ingredients, with sea salt and freshly ground black pepper to taste.

3   Pat dry the chicken skin, sprinkle with flaky sea salt and black pepper, and rub with a drizzle of olive oil. Add half the stuffing mixture to the cavity, followed by the garlic bulb to seal – this will prevent the chickpeas from falling out while cooking. Set aside the remaining stuffing mixture.

4   Roast the chicken in the oven for 20 minutes, then lower the oven temperature to 180°C (350°F) Gas Mark 4 and roast for a further 1 hour until golden and crispy on the outside and still juicy on the inside. Add the remaining stuffing mixture to the tin around the chicken 20 minutes before the end of the cooking time. When cooked through, the chicken's internal temperature should read around 75°C (167°F).

5   While the chicken is cooking, prepare the salsa verde. Add the coriander, parsley, olive oil, lemon zest and juice, and garlic to a bowl, with sea salt and black pepper to taste, and mix.

6   Remove the chicken from the oven and scoop out the chickpeas from inside and around the chicken into a bowl. Leave the chicken to rest for 10 minutes to reabsorb all of the beautiful juices.

7   Squeeze the roasted garlic into the bowl of chickpeas, pour in any leftover chicken juices then mash it all up with the back of a fork, leaving some chunks in there for texture. Add a splash of hot water to help mash the chickpeas, if needed.

8   Carve the chicken and serve with the lemon and herb chickpeas on the side, and a drizzle of salsa verde over the top. This goes nicely with the mini roast potatoes on page 186.

TWICE-BAKED CHEDDAR SOUFFLÉ

I first had this a few years ago on my birthday at a pub near to where I grew up. Since then, it has been my go-to whenever I see it on a menu. This recipe has been created with those memories in mind. I can guarantee you, you will not regret making it.

SERVES 4

25g (2 tbsp) unsalted butter, plus extra for greasing
50g (6½ tbsp) plain (all-purpose) flour
250ml (9fl oz) cold whole milk
A few gratings of nutmeg
½ tsp Dijon mustard
50g (2oz) Cheddar, grated
50g (2oz) Gouda, grated, plus extra to finish
2 large egg yolks
3 large egg whites (roughly 125g/4½oz)
1 tsp lemon juice

For the creamed spinach
4 small shallots, sliced
Large knob of butter (about 4 tbsp)
5 garlic cloves, grated
400ml (1¾ cups) double (heavy) cream
1 tsp Dijon mustard
300g (10½oz) frozen spinach
120ml (8 tbsp) water

Note: Save the third egg yolk to make custard (see page 221) or add it to scrambled eggs.

1 Melt the butter in a pan over a medium heat, then mix in the flour to form a paste. Gradually add the milk, continuously whisking, until it has all been incorporated. Leave to cook for a few minutes, then remove from the heat and mix in the nutmeg, mustard, cheeses and egg yolks and season with sea salt and freshly ground black pepper. Stir until the cheese has completely melted, then tip into a large mixing bowl and leave to cool.

2 Meanwhile, prepare the creamed spinach. Add the shallots to a wide ovenproof frying pan with the butter. Fry for 10 minutes over a medium-high heat until starting to caramelize. Add the garlic, turn the heat down to medium and cook for a few more minutes until softened. Add the cream, mustard, frozen spinach and water, with sea salt and black pepper to taste. Cover with a lid and cook for 5 minutes until all the spinach has defrosted, then remove the lid and cook for 10 minutes until the sauce has thickened slightly and the spinach has broken up a bit. Remove from the heat and set aside.

3 Preheat the oven to 180°C (350°F) Gas Mark 4. Generously grease the inside of a large 12cm (5in) soufflé dish with butter.

4 Add the lemon juice and egg whites to a large bowl and beat with an electric whisk for 5–10 minutes until stiff peaks form.

5 Gently fold the egg whites into the cooled cheese mixture, in three batches. The first batch of egg whites can be folded in a little more vigorously as the cheese mixture will have solidified.

6 Pour the soufflé mixture into the prepared dish and place the dish on a baking tray. Cook in the oven for 30–35 minutes until risen, browned on top and cooked through. Remove the soufflé from the oven (leaving it turned on) and set aside to cool and deflate (about 10 minutes) before using a knife around the edges to help remove it from the dish.

7 Place the cooled soufflé on top of the creamed spinach in the ovenproof frying pan. Spoon over some of the creamed spinach, then top with a small grating of Gouda. Place the pan in the oven for a final 10–15 minutes until the cheese has melted and the soufflé has warmed through.

CHICKEN WINGS – TWO WAYS

The secret to a great chicken wing is the combination of flours used in the coating. Double frying them gives you an extremely crispy exterior. However, if you're rushed for time, a single fry for a few minutes extra will work. I love both these sauces so much, I couldn't chose between them. The recipes take their influence from two of my favourite cuisines — Mexican and Vietnamese. Feel free to use them as a coating, as I do here, or as a dip on the side.

SERVES 6

80g (⅔ cup) cornflour (cornstarch)
180g (1½ cups) plain (all-purpose) flour
1 tsp fine sea salt
Vegetable oil, for deep-frying
2kg (4½lb) chicken wings

1   Mix the flours and salt in a bowl.

2   Add enough oil to come a third of the way up the sides of a heavy-based saucepan and heat to 160°C (320°F).

3   In batches, place the chicken wings in the flour and toss to coat. Shake off any excess flour from the wings and lower carefully into the oil. Cook for 3 minutes then remove from the oil, using a slotted spoon, and place on a wire rack.

4   Turn the heat up and bring the oil up to 180°C (356°F). Place the chicken back in the flour, lightly coating a second time, then fry in the hot oil for 4–5 minutes until crispy and cooked through. After each batch, place the wings on a rack set over a baking tray, and keep warm in a low oven.

5   Remove the chicken from the oven and toss in a bowl with your sauce of choice.

**MAKES 400G (14OZ)
ENOUGH FOR 1KG
(2LB 4OZ) CHICKEN WINGS**

FOR THE JALAPEÑO SAUCE

10 jalapeño chillies (200g/7oz
   in total), stalks removed and
   chillies cut in half (seeds can be
   removed for a mild sauce)
½ onion
5 garlic cloves, peeled
Large bunch of coriander (cilantro)
1 tsp caster (superfine) sugar
Juice of 4 limes
60ml (scant ⅓ cup) vegetable oil

1   Place the jalapeños, onion and garlic on a roasting tray and place under
a hot grill (broiler) for 5–6 minutes until charred. Tip into a blender, add
the coriander, sugar and lime juice, with sea salt to taste, and blitz on high
until smooth.

2   To finish the sauce, gradually stream in the oil while the blender is on high
until everything has emulsified and mixed together. Store in an airtight
bottle, in the fridge, for up to 2 weeks.

3   To serve, heat up the sauce, place the cooked wings in a bowl, pour over
some of the sauce and toss until combined.

**MAKES 400G (14OZ)
ENOUGH FOR 1KG
(2LB 4OZ) CHICKEN WINGS**

FOR THE NƯỚC CHẤM SAUCE

150ml (⅔ cup) water
Juice of 2 small limes (6 tbsp)
100ml (3½fl oz) fish sauce
150g (⅔ cup) caster (superfine)
   sugar
2 small lemongrass stalks, finely
   chopped (20g/¾oz)
5 garlic cloves, minced
2 red chillies, finely chopped
Large handful of roasted peanuts,
   to garnish

1   Add the water, lime juice, fish sauce, sugar, lemongrass, garlic and chilli
to a pan. Bring to a boil over a medium-high heat and bubble away for
15–20 minutes, until thicker and syrup-like.

2   Remove from the heat and set aside until ready to use, heating it through
before you serve.

3   Add the sauce and wings to a bowl, toss until combined, sprinkle over the
roasted peanuts and serve.

PAPRIKA PRAWNS ON SOURDOUGH TOAST/154

CRISPY PORK BELLY BITES WITH APPLE SAUCE/157

HASSELBACK PATATAS BRAVAS/158

MUSHROOM & TRUFFLE ARANCINI/161

CHICKEN SATAY WITH SPICY PEANUT SAUCE/162

FRENCH ONION FLATBREAD/165

THAI-STYLE FISHCAKES/166

SPINACH & FETA FILO PARCELS/169

KOREAN FRIED POPCORN CHICKEN/170

CHORIZO CROQUETTES/171

ONION BHAJIS/173

TUNA & CRISPY RICE BITES/174

COURGETTE & FETA FRITTERS/177

GRILLED LAMB CHOPS WITH SALSA VERDE/178

SHARING PLATES

05

PAPRIKA PRAWNS ON SOURDOUGH TOAST

This is one of those dishes that you simply won't be able to stop craving. Inspired by the flavours of Portugese cuisine, the prawns are marinated and fried, then served on sourdough. My favourite thing about this recipe is eating the bread at the end that has soaked up all the escaped juices.

SERVES 2

325g (11½oz) raw king prawns (jumbo shrimp), shelled (prepared weight)
3 tbsp olive oil, plus extra for brushing
80ml (⅓ cup) water
2–4 slices of sourdough bread
1–2 garlic cloves, peeled
Finely chopped flat-leaf parsley, to garnish

For the marinade
4 garlic cloves, minced
2 tbsp smoked paprika
1 tbsp fennel seeds, crushed
4 tbsp olive oil
½ tbsp honey
Bunch of flat-leaf parsley, leaves finely chopped

1 Mix the prawns with the marinade ingredients, adding sea salt and freshly ground black pepper to taste. Cover and place in the fridge to marinate for at least a few hours, or ideally overnight.

2 Heat the olive oil in a sauté pan over a high heat and add the prawns. Fry for 3–4 minutes until pink and cooked through. Remove the prawns from the pan, leaving behind as much of the marinade as possible, then add the water. Mix together and reduce until the sauce has thickened slightly.

3 While the sauce is reducing, brush the sourdough slices with some olive oil and toast in a griddle pan on both sides until golden. Rub each slice of sourdough with a garlic clove (up to ½ a clove per slice, depending on how fragrant you want it to be).

4 Spoon the prawns on top of the sourdough, drizzle with the reduced sauce and top with parsley to serve.

CRISPY PORK BELLY BITES WITH APPLE SAUCE

A sharing plate version of the notorious crispy pork belly. Pricking the skin, salting it and brushing it with vinegar are all vital steps for achieving that crisp, golden skin we all love.

SERVES 4–6

1kg (2¼lb) pork belly (unscored)
2 tbsp flaky sea salt
2 tbsp white wine vinegar

For the pork rub
2 tbsp fennel seeds, crushed
2 tsp dried chilli flakes
1 tbsp brown sugar

For the apple sauce
Large knob of butter (about 2 tbsp)
½ white onion, finely diced
5 cooking apples, peeled, cored
  and diced
150ml (⅔ cup) water
2 cloves

1   Completely dry the pork using kitchen paper. Using a sharp knife, prick holes all over the skin; the more holes, the crisper it will be. Be careful not to go too deep and cut the meat itself; only break the surface of the skin.

2   Mix the pork rub ingredients together with some freshly ground black pepper, flip the pork upside down and massage the rub into the meat. Make sure you don't get any on top of the pork skin. Place the pork, skin side up, on some foil, then wrap this tightly around the edges so that only the skin is showing. Tip the flaky sea salt onto the skin and spread it out evenly so all of the skin is covered. Leave the pork to sit in the fridge, lightly covered, for 24 hours, or at least overnight.

3   When ready to cook, preheat the oven to 140°C (275°F) Gas Mark 1.

4   Remove the pork from the fridge and scrape off any remaining salt. Pat the skin completely dry using kitchen paper, then brush some of the vinegar onto the skin (this helps it crisp). Place the pork, still in the foil, onto a rack on a roasting tray and transfer to the oven for 2½ hours.

5   Meanwhile, make the apple sauce. Add the butter and onion to a saucepan over a medium-high heat and cook for 10 minutes until the onion has softened. Add the apples, water and cloves, and season with sea salt and freshly ground black pepper. Cover with a lid and cook for 25–30 minutes over a medium-low heat, stirring regularly to prevent the sauce from sticking, until the apple has broken down. Remove the cloves and blend the sauce until smooth, then set aside.

6   Remove the pork from the oven and unwrap it from the foil bundle. Place the pork back on the rack on the roasting tray, brush some more vinegar onto the skin, then place under a grill (broiler) on high for 5–10 minutes until golden and crisp. Keep an eye on it as you don't want the skin to burn.

7   Remove the pork from the grill, and leave to rest for a few minutes.

8   Cut the pork belly into cubes, then serve with the apple sauce.

HASSELBACK PATATAS BRAVAS

Here I've gone for a twist on Spanish patatas bravas. The addition of crumbled feta helps cut through the rich flavours of the sauces.

MAKES 10

10 small white potatoes (such as Maris Piper), scrubbed
2 tbsp olive oil
100g (⅔ cup) crumbled feta

For the bravas sauce
30ml (2 tbsp) olive oil
2 tbsp smoked paprika, plus extra to garnish
1 tbsp plain (all-purpose) flour
200ml (scant 1 cup) chicken stock
1 tsp red wine vinegar
1 tsp honey
10 dashes of Tabasco

For the garlic sauce
1 garlic clove, grated
40g (2¾ tbsp) mayonnaise
100g (scant ½ cup) sour cream

1   Preheat the oven to 200°C (400°F) Gas Mark 6.

2   Cut thin slices into the potatoes, making sure not to cut all the way through. The more slices you can do, the better. Use two wooden spoons or chopsticks placed either side of the potato to help prevent cutting all the way through.

3   Place the potatoes in a baking tray, drizzle with the olive oil, season with sea salt, then roast in the oven for 1 hour until golden, crisp and cooked through.

4   Meanwhile, make the bravas sauce. Add the oil to a saucepan over a low heat. Add the paprika, mix thoroughly, then add the flour and mix. Cook for 30 seconds more.

5   Gradually add the chicken stock, stirring continuously, then add the vinegar, honey and Tabasco (two non-authentic ingredients but very welcome additions, in my opinion). Season with sea salt and simmer over a medium-low heat for 5 minutes until thickened.

6   To make the garlic sauce, mix the ingredients together in a bowl, adding sea salt to taste.

7   Remove the potatoes from the oven, lay them on a plate, drizzle with the bravas and garlic sauces, and scatter the feta over the top. Sprinkle with some more paprika to serve.

MUSHROOM & TRUFFLE ARANCINI

This has to be the hero of all sharing plates and is a big crowd pleaser. It is also a great way of using up leftover risotto from page 59. Make sure to sprinkle the arancini with a little truffle salt straight after cooking, to add the perfect salty finish.

MAKES 12

600g (1lb 5oz) chilled mushroom risotto (leftover from recipe on page 59)
Vegetable oil, for deep-frying
50g (scant ½ cup) plain (all-purpose) flour
2 eggs, beaten
200g (4 cups) panko breadcrumbs
Truffle salt, to garnish

For the garlic-truffle mayonnaise
2 garlic cloves, minced
6 tbsp mayonnaise
2 pinches of smoked paprika
Squeeze of lemon juice
2 tbsp truffle oil

1   Scoop out 1 heaped tablespoon of chilled risotto (roughly 50g/1¾oz) and roll into a ball in your hands. Repeat with the rest of the mixture, then place all the balls in the freezer to quickly chill.

2   Meanwhile, to make the garlic-truffle mayonnaise, mix all the ingredients together in a bowl and season with sea salt and freshly ground black pepper. Chill until ready to use.

3   Third-fill a heavy-based pan with vegetable oil, then heat the oil to 165°C (329°F).

4   Place the flour, eggs and panko breadcrumbs in separate shallow bowls. Remove the arancini balls from the freezer and, one at a time, roll lightly in the flour, shaking off excess, then roll in the egg, followed by the breadcrumbs.

5   In batches, deep-fry the arancini in the hot oil for 4 minutes until lightly golden brown. Remove and place on a wire rack.

6   Increase the heat of the oil to 180°C (356°F) and deep-fry the arancini for another 3 minutes until golden brown and crisp. Lift out of the oil onto kitchen paper to absorb any excess oil.

7   Sprinkle with truffle salt and serve with the delicious garlic mayonnaise.

CHICKEN SATAY WITH SPICY PEANUT SAUCE

Chicken satay is a delicious Southeast Asian dish that is perfect for enjoying with others. Marinating the chicken and soaking the skewers are both vital steps. If you can, grilling the chicken over coals will add an extra smoky flavour to the dish.

MAKES 18–20 SKEWERS

1kg (2lb 4oz) boneless and skinless chicken thighs, cut into bite-sized pieces
Lime wedges, to serve

For the marinade
30g (1oz) lemongrass stalk
4 tsp coriander seeds
½ tsp ground turmeric
4 tbsp olive oil
4 tbsp water
6 garlic cloves, grated

For the spicy peanut sauce
1 tbsp gochujang paste
100g (generous ⅓ cup) smooth peanut butter
2 garlic cloves, minced
2 tbsp light soy sauce
1 tsp curry powder
6 tbsp water
2 tbsp olive oil

1   You will need 18–20 bamboo skewers, each 15cm (6 inches) long.

2   Add the marinade ingredients to a blender with sea salt and freshly ground black pepper to taste. Blitz together until smooth then transfer to a large bowl.

3   Add the chicken to the marinade, cover and leave to marinate in the fridge for a few hours. Meanwhile, soak the wooden skewers in some water to stop them from burning when grilling. If using metal skewers, you don't need to soak them.

4   To make the spicy peanut sauce, mix all the ingredients together in a bowl, check for seasoning and adjust to your preference.

5   When ready to cook, remove the chicken from the fridge and take the skewers out of the water. Thread the pieces of chicken onto the skewers tightly and place under the grill (broiler) on high. Cook for 6–7 minutes on each side until there is a nice char on the outside. If the skewers start burning, cover the ends with foil.

6   Serve with the spicy peanut sauce and a squeeze of lime juice.

FRENCH ONION FLATBREADS

French onion soup is fantastic, but have you tried French onion flatbreads?! This is a riff on the classic soup, turning it into another meal that is so comforting and delicious, and the perfect weekend treat.

MAKES 4

1 quantity of pitta dough
   (see page 105)
1 tbsp butter
2 tbsp olive oil
4 large onions, sliced
2 tbsp finely chopped thyme leaves
400ml (1¾ cups) beef stock
80g (1 cup) fresh breadcrumbs
2 tbsp olive oil, plus extra for
   drizzling
2 tbsp finely chopped rosemary
240g (8½oz) Gruyère, grated
Handful of parsley, leaves roughly
   chopped, to garnish

Note: If using a kitchen oven, turn a baking sheet upside down and place it in the oven to preheat, too. This acts as a pizza stone (if you don't have one) and works very well for dishes like this.

1   Prepare the pitta dough, and leave to prove while preparing the rest of the ingredients.

2   Add the butter, olive oil, onions and thyme to a sauté pan over a medium-high heat. Season with some sea salt and freshly ground black pepper, cover with a lid and cook for 5 minutes until starting to turn translucent and brown.

3   Reduce the heat to medium-low, pour in the stock, cover with a lid and cook for 20 minutes.

4   Uncover the pan and cook the onions for a final 10 minutes until they reach a thick consistency. Check for seasoning and set aside to cool.

5   Preheat the oven to 200°C (400°F) Gas Mark 6.

6   Put the breadcrumbs in a bowl with the olive oil and rosemary, and season. Mix well until all breadcrumbs are coated, tip them onto a roasting tray and cook in the oven for 5 minutes until starting to turn golden. Remove from the oven and set aside to cool.

7   Increase the oven temperature to 220°C (425°F) Gas Mark 7 or preheat your pizza oven (see Note).

8   Once the dough has doubled in size, knock the air out and divide into 4 balls. Using your hands, stretch the dough out into the shape of a small pizza. If the dough is resistant, leave the portions to rest for 20 minutes covered with a tea (dish) towel.

9   Spread the cooled onions onto the flatbreads, then top with the grated Gruyère. Sprinkle over some of the toasted breadcrumbs and drizzle with a little bit of olive oil. Brush the edges of the flatbread with some oil as well. Cook them in the pizza oven for 1–2 minutes, or slide them onto the preheated baking tray in the kitchen oven and cook for 6–7 minutes.

10 Serve with a sprinkling of fresh parsley and enjoy.

THAI-STYLE FISHCAKES

Although not entirely authentic, this is my version of wonderful Thai fishcakes. Coating them in rice flour before frying gives an extra crispy exterior. This is a great sharing platter that will go down well with everyone.

MAKES 20

2 x 2.5cm (1inch) knobs of fresh root ginger, peeled and roughly chopped

3 large lemongrass stalks, roughly chopped

700g (1lb 9oz) skinless cod fillets (any plain white fish is fine)

2 large bunches of coriander (cilantro), leaves only

Grated zest and juice of 2 limes

5 tbsp fish sauce

4 red chillies, deseeded

4 garlic cloves, peeled

6 tbsp rice flour, plus extra for coating

2 tbsp cold water

Vegetable oil, for shallow-frying

Sweet chilli dipping sauce, to serve

1   Add the ginger and lemongrass to a small blender or spice grinder and blend on high until a paste has formed. This step is not essential, but helps when blending these ingredients with the rest. If you skip it, chop them both up into small pieces instead.

2   Place the ginger and lemongrass in a regular sized blender. Add the remaining ingredients except the water, oil and dipping sauce and blend on high until a smooth paste has formed.

3   Still with the blender on high, very gradually stream in the cold water to help lock some moisture into the paste.

4   With damp hands, separate the paste into 20 portions (about 50g/2oz each). Roll each portion into a ball, press down slightly to form a thick disc, then gently roll in some rice flour.

5   Heat a 2.5cm (1-inch) depth of oil in a deep frying pan over a medium-high heat. To test, drop in a crumb of the fishcake mixture and if it bubbles, you can start cooking. In batches, shallow-fry the fishcakes for 2–3 minutes on each side, until cooked through and a crisp exterior has formed. Remove from the oil using a slotted spoon and place on kitchen paper to absorb excess oil.

6   Sprinkle with flaky sea salt and serve with a sweet chilli dipping sauce.

SPINACH & FETA FILO PARCELS

A delicious Greek spanakopita parcel. Feta and spinach make a well-known and winning combination. By turning the classic dish into parcels and using shop-bought filo pastry, they become so quick and easy to make. They would taste delicious dipped in homemade tzatziki (see page 107).

MAKES 8

1 tbsp olive oil, plus extra for brushing
1 onion, diced
2 garlic cloves, minced
250g (9oz) baby leaf spinach
Handful (1 tbsp) of mint leaves
Grated zest and juice of ½ lemon
1 egg
200g (7oz) feta, roughly broken into clumps
4 sheets of filo (phyllo) pastry, halved lengthways (roughly 12.5cm/5inches wide)

1 Add the olive oil to a pan over a medium heat and fry the onion for 10 minutes until softened. Add the garlic and cook for a few more minutes.

2 Meanwhile, bring a pan of water to the boil and blanch the spinach for 30 seconds. Drain and transfer to a bowl of iced water to cool, then remove and squeeze out any excess liquid from the spinach using your hands.

3 Place the spinach, onion and garlic, mint, lemon zest and juice, egg and feta in a blender. Add sea salt and freshly ground black pepper to taste, bearing in mind the feta is quite salty. Pulse until roughly chopped and mixed but not too smooth – we still want there to be some chunks of feta and spinach throughout.

4 Preheat the oven to 170°C (340°F) Gas Mark 3½.

5 Using a damp tea (dish) towel to cover the sheets you are not working with so they don't dry out, lay a strip of filo out flat and brush it lightly with olive oil. Place 2 tablespoons of the filling in the bottom corner, and fold over onto itself into a triangle. Keep folding over until the length of the pastry has been used. Brush olive oil on top, place on a baking tray and repeat with the remaining filo and filling, using a second baking tray if needed, to avoiding overcrowding.

6 Bake in the oven for 25 minutes until golden brown and crisp.

KOREAN FRIED POPCORN CHICKEN

Serving this alongside some well-seasoned sushi rice (see page 201) and crunchy lettuce leaves would make it a lovely meal to enjoy with others.

SERVES 4–6

300ml (1⅓ cups) buttermilk
3½ tbsp gochujang paste
640g (1lb 6½oz) boneless and skinless chicken thighs, cut into bite-sized pieces
1½ tbsp sesame seeds
5 garlic cloves, grated
4 tbsp sesame oil
1 tbsp rice wine vinegar (or apple cider vinegar)
1½ tbsp honey
3 tbsp light soy sauce
Vegetable oil, for deep-frying
300g (2½ cups) plain (all-purpose) flour
½ tsp fine sea salt
2 spring onions (scallions), julienned

1   Mix the buttermilk with ½ tablespoon of the gochujang in a bowl. Add the chicken to the marinade and mix. Cover and leave to marinate in the fridge overnight, or for a few hours at least. The acidity in the buttermilk helps tenderize the chicken.

2   Add the sesame seeds to a dry pan and toast over a medium heat until golden brown.

3   To prepare the sauce, add the remaining gochujang to a saucepan with the garlic, sesame oil, vinegar, honey, soy sauce and toasted sesame seeds. Place over a medium-low heat and cook for 10 minutes until thickened and sticky, stirring frequently. Remove from the heat and set aside. This can be stored in the fridge for a week.

4   Add vegetable oil to a deep, heavy-based pan to come halfway up the sides of the pan, and heat to 180°C (356°F). Tip the flour and salt into a bowl and mix, then remove the chicken from the fridge.

5   Lift the pieces of chicken out of the buttermilk and place in the bowl of flour. Toss to coat, pressing the flour into the chicken to get a good coating, then carefully lower them into the hot oil, in batches. Fry for 7 minutes until golden and crisp, then place the cooked pieces on a wire rack set over a baking tray and keep warm in a low oven.

6   Meanwhile, reheat the sauce then tip into a large mixing bowl. Add the fried chicken and toss to evenly coat.

7   Lay the chicken out on a platter and top with the spring onions to serve.

CHORIZO CROQUETTES

These aren't traditional, but they are certainly delicious. They are best dipped in homemade garlic sauce (see page 158).

MAKES 16

75g (2½oz) chorizo, diced into small pieces
2 tbsp unsalted butter
120g (1 cup) plain (all-purpose) flour
350ml (1½ cups) cold whole milk
80g (2¾oz) shredded mozzarella cheese
Vegetable oil, for frying

To coat
100g (¾ cup) plain (all-purpose) flour
2 eggs, beaten together
200g (4 cups) panko breadcrumbs
1 large bunch of thyme, stalks removed, leaves finely chopped

1   Place the chorizo in a cold pan and cook over a medium heat for 5 minutes. Remove from the heat and set aside.

2   Meanwhile, place the butter in a pan and cook over a medium heat for 4 minutes until browned. Just before it has fully browned, turn the heat down low so it doesn't burn and add the flour. Mix the butter and flour together, then gradually pour in the milk while continuously whisking.

3   Once the milk has been incorporated, turn the heat up to medium and bring the sauce to a gentle bubble. Cook for 5 minutes.

4   Turn off the heat, add the chorizo and mozzarella and stir until melted and combined. Cover the pan with a lid and set aside to cool to room temperature.

5   Once cooled, transfer the mixture into a piping bag with a 2cm (¾ inch) nozzle. Pipe the mixture into rows on a parchment-lined baking tray. Place the croquettes into the freezer for 3 hours.

6   To coat the croquettes, place the flour in a wide bowl, the beaten egg in another, and combine the breadcrumbs and thyme in a third bowl.

7   Half-fill a heavy-based pan with vegetable oil and heat to 170°C (340°F). Preheat the oven to 120°C (250°F) Gas Mark ½.

8   Cut the rows into roughly 5cm (2inch) pieces (30g/1oz), then coat evenly in the flour. Shake off any excess, then dip in the egg mixture, followed by the breadcrumbs. Make sure each croquette is evenly coated in breadcrumbs, then dip back into the egg, then back into the breadcrumbs for a final coating. This double coating will ensure no sauce leaks from them while frying.

9   Cook the croquettes in batches in the hot oil for 5 minutes until golden and crisp.

10 Lift out with a slotted spoon, shake off excess oil, then place onto a rack set over a baking tray. Place the baking tray in the preheated oven to keep the croquettes warm while frying the rest.

ONION BHAJIS

It wasn't until I spent some time in India that I learnt the game-changing trick for making incredibly light, crispy and flavoursome bhajis. Make sure to properly squeeze the onions at the start and leave them to rest for the full amount of designated time to draw out the moisture. This oniony liquid will help bring the bhajis together without the need for water.

MAKES 9

2 onions, finely sliced
   (250–300g/9–10½oz prepared
   weight)
1 small green chilli, finely chopped
Bunch of coriander (cilantro),
   leaves finely chopped
2 garlic cloves, minced
Small pinch of ground turmeric
1 tsp ground coriander
2 tsp ground cumin
25g (1oz) gram (chickpea) flour
Vegetable oil, for shallow-frying

For the yogurt chutney
4 tbsp thick Greek yogurt
Handful of mint, leaves only
Bunch of coriander (cilantro),
   leaves only
Small squeeze of lemon juice

1 Season the onions with sea salt and mix together, squeezing them in your hands to help release their juices. Leave to sit for 30 minutes to draw out some excess moisture.

2 Meanwhile, to make the yogurt chutney, add all the ingredients to a blender, with sea salt to taste, and blitz until completely smooth. Check for seasoning and adjust accordingly. Transfer to a bowl and set aside.

3 Add the chilli, coriander, garlic and spices to the onions. Mix them around again, squeezing them with your hands, until more juices start coming out. Add the flour and thoroughly mix one more time. The mixture should stick together slightly, but shouldn't be overly sticky. This way, the bhajis will stay light and crispy.

4 Heat a 1.5cm (⅝-inch) depth of oil in a deep frying pan over a medium-high heat and spoon 30g (1oz) portions of the bhaji mixture into the oil. Shallow-fry for 2–3 minutes on each side until golden and crisp.

5 Remove the bhajis from the oil and place on kitchen paper to absorb excess oil.

6 Sprinkle with flaky sea salt and serve with the yogurt chutney.

TUNA & CRISPY RICE BITES

This recipe is my take on Nobu's viral spicy salmon on crispy rice, with an alternative ahi-tuna-poke-inspired topping. The combination of macadamia nuts, rich tuna, salty soy sauce and raw onion makes for a delicious topping to the crispy rice. A grating of lime zest at the end is a lovely way to finish.

MAKES ABOUT 24 BITES

300g (10½oz) sushi rice
300ml (10fl oz) water
50ml (scant ¼ cup) rice vinegar
20g (1½ tbsp) caster (superfine) sugar
300g (10½oz) sushi-grade tuna, cut into small cubes (ask your fishmonger for tuna to eat raw and they should be able to help)
½ small onion, finely diced
1 × 2.5cm (1inch) knob of fresh root ginger, grated
20g (¾oz) macadamia nuts, toasted and crushed
1½ tbsp sesame seeds, toasted
3 tsp sesame oil
2 tbsp soy sauce
Vegetable oil, for shallow-frying
Grated lime zest, to serve
Sliced spring onions, to serve

Note: When frying the rice, don't move it around in the oil or it will fall apart; be careful.

1   Start by cooking the sushi rice and rice seasoning according to the instructions on page 201.

2   Tip the rice out onto a baking tray lined with clingfilm (plastic wrap), flatten the surface, lightly compact down into the tray a bit, then fold over the clingfilm to cover and place in the freezer for at least 1 hour until firm, or frozen if left in longer.

3   Meanwhile, in a bowl, mix the tuna, onion, ginger, macadamia nuts, sesame seeds, sesame oil and soy sauce. Cover and leave to marinate in the fridge while preparing the rice.

4   Once the rice is firm or frozen, carefully tip the rice out of the tray and use a damp knife to cut into bite-sized pieces.

5   Heat enough vegetable oil for shallow-frying in a deep frying pan over a medium-high heat. Add the rice pieces and shallow-fry for 4–5 minutes until golden and crispy (see Note below).

6   Once cooked, remove from the oil, sprinkle with sea salt and top with the tuna. Garnish with a grating of lime zest and some sliced spring onions to serve.

COURGETTE & FETA FRITTERS

The stand-out element of this dish, for me, is the feta. When it is incorporated into these Greek-style fritters, the feta softens and almost melts into the fritter itself. These would go really well with homemade tzatziki (see page 107).

MAKES 10–12

2 courgettes (zucchini), grated
   (325g/11½oz in total)
40g (⅓ cup) plain (all-purpose) flour
2 eggs
150g (5½oz) feta
Vegetable oil, for shallow-frying

1 Grate the courgettes, place them in a tea (dish) towel then squeeze out as much moisture from them as possible. If you have time, mix the courgettes with a small pinch of sea salt, place in a mesh strainer over the top of a bowl and leave to dry out in the fridge overnight. When you get back to these, you will see how just how much moisture has been removed and how this step helps prevent them from being too watery.

2 Add the courgettes to a bowl with the flour, eggs and some freshly ground black pepper. Mix thoroughly then crumble in the feta. Mix again to combine.

3 Add a 2.5cm (1-inch) depth of oil to a deep frying pan and heat to a medium-high heat.

4 When the oil is hot, spoon in heaped tablespoons of the mix and fry for 3 minutes on each side until golden brown. Remove the fritters from the pan and place on kitchen paper to absorb excess oil.

5 Sprinkle with flaky sea salt while they are still hot and serve.

GRILLED LAMB CHOPS WITH SALSA VERDE

This dish is the epitome of a weekend feast. Buying a whole rack of lamb, breaking it up into cutlets and grilling them over some coals would make a wonderful sharing platter for family and friends. You could also serve this with some purple sprouting broccoli, buttery new potatoes or the creamy mashed potato on page 71.

MAKES 7

1 x 350g (12oz) rack of lamb (with 7 cutlets on), cutlets cut apart and separated
8 tbsp thick Greek yogurt
Bunch of flat-leaf parsley, leaves chopped

For the marinade
1 tbsp olive oil
2 garlic cloves, grated
Sprig of rosemary, needles finely chopped
¼ tsp ground cinnamon
1 tsp dried oregano

For the salsa verde
20 basil leaves (2 bunches)
2 garlic cloves, minced
20g (¾oz) coriander (cilantro) leaves
2 big squeezes of lemon juice
160ml (generous ¾ cup) olive oil

1   Mix the marinade ingredients together in a large bowl, add the lamb chops and mix until evenly coated. Cover and leave to marinate for a few hours.

2   Meanwhile, prepare the salsa verde. In a pestle and mortar (or a hand-held blender if preferred), crush everything together except for the oil. Once you have a green paste, mix in the oil and add sea salt to taste.

3   Heat a lightly oiled griddle pan (or BBQ/grill) to high. Add the lamb chops and cook for 4 minutes on each side. Remove and leave to rest for 5 minutes before serving.

4   Spoon the Greek yogurt onto a plate and spread it out with the back of a spoon. Place the rested lamb chops on top, drizzle with the salsa verde, and top with a sprinkling of flaky sea salt and parsley.

ASPARAGUS, PEA & CRISPY QUINOA SALAD/182

'NDUJA & BACON HISPI CABBAGE/185

MINI ROSEMARY ROAST POTATOES/186

FENNEL & PEACH SALAD/188

ROCKET, FIG & BURRATA SALAD/189

QUICK KIMCHI-INSPIRED SALAD/192

ROASTED SQUASH WITH SALSA MACHA/195

CHICORY, BLUE CHEESE & GRAPEFRUIT SALAD/196

MISO AUBERGINE/199

BUTTERY-SPICED BASMATI RICE/200

CHEESY POLENTA/200

SUSHI RICE/201

ROSEMARY & THYME FRIES/201

TENDERSTEM BROCCOLI WITH TAHINI DRESSING/203

HERBY POTATO & CAVOLO NERO GRATIN/204

SIDES & SALADS

06

ASPARAGUS, PEA & CRISPY QUINOA SALAD

Fresh peas are key here, as they are far more tender than frozen ones. Don't be put off by the sound of crispy quinoa – this gives an amazing textural difference to the dish and adds a lovely nuttiness to its fresh and bright flavours.

SERVES 2 AS A SIDE

250g (9oz) asparagus, cut on an angle into 2.5cm (1-inch) lengths
½ tbsp olive oil
75g (3 oz) quinoa
375ml (1⅔ cup) vegetable stock
100g (3½oz) shelled peas (ideally fresh)

For the dressing
2 tbsp mint leaves, finely chopped
2 tbsp olive oil
1 tsp Dijon mustard
1 garlic clove, peeled

1   Preheat the oven to 180°C (350°F) Gas Mark 4.

2   Place the asparagus in a roasting tray with the olive oil and season with sea salt. Roast in the oven for 15–20 minutes until golden brown, but not too soft and overcooked. Remove from the oven and leave to cool, and increase the oven temperature to 200°C (400°F) Gas Mark 6.

3   While the asparagus is roasting, rinse the quinoa under cold water then place in a saucepan with the stock. Bring to the boil and cook for 20 minutes until cooked through and all the stock has been absorbed. Drain, leave to steam-dry for a few minutes, then tip out onto a baking tray and spread it out over the tray.

4   Cook the quinoa in the oven for 10 minutes until it has dried out, browned and crisped up. Remove from the oven and set aside to cool.

5   Remove all the peas from their pods, bring a pan of salted water to a boil, tip in the peas and blanch for 3 minutes. Drain and place in a bowl of ice-cold water to cool. Once cooled, drain and spread out on kitchen paper to dry.

6   To make the dressing add the ingredients with a pinch of sea salt to a small blender and blitz until smooth and combined.

7   When ready to serve, add the quinoa, asparagus and peas to a bowl and pour over the dressing. Give it a good mix together, then serve.

'NDUJA & BACON HISPI CABBAGE

Cabbage doesn't need to be boring, especially when seared and served with a delicious, creamy bacon sauce. This works well as a side dish alongside a light main course, or can even be eaten as a main dish by itself.

SERVES 2

1 sweetheart or hispi cabbage, outer leaves removed
2 tbsp olive oil
160g (5½oz) bacon lardons
2 tbsp 'nduja paste
Knob of butter (about 2 tbsp)
150ml (⅔ cup) chicken stock
2 tbsp double (heavy) cream

1 Place a frying pan over a medium-high heat.

2 Cut the cabbage in half, and in half again, so you have 4 quarters. Coat the cabbage in the olive oil, rubbing it in to make sure all surfaces are covered.

3 Place the cabbage in the pan and fry both flat sides for 5 minutes each until they are nicely charred. Remove from the pan and turn the heat down to medium.

4 Add the bacon lardons to the pan, cook for 10 minutes until crispy, then remove and set aside. Add the 'nduja and butter to the pan, season with freshly ground black pepper and bring the sauce to a foamy bubble.

5 Return the cabbage pieces to the pan, flat side down, and baste for 2 minutes.

6 Add the stock and cream, cover with a lid and braise for 10–12 minutes, turning the cabbage pieces halfway through.

7 When the sauce has reduced and the cabbage is cooked through and tender, transfer to a large plate. Drizzle with the sauce and sprinkle over the crispy bacon and serve.

MINI ROSEMARY ROAST POTATOES

The key here is to make sure the potatoes are left to steam-dry after boiling. That way, the exterior will become extra crispy and golden. These are delicious served with grilled or slow-roasted meats.

SERVES 4 AS A SIDE

700g (1lb 9oz) potatoes
3 tbsp goose or duck fat
6 garlic cloves, unpeeled
2 large sprigs of rosemary

For the rosemary salt
2 sprigs of rosemary, needles finely chopped
1 tbsp flaky sea salt
Grated zest of 1 lemon

1   Peel (if you like) the potatoes, and cut into cubes, roughly 2cm (¾inch). Bring a large pan of salted water to the boil and add the potatoes. Boil for 5–6 minutes until soft. Drain in a colander and leave to steam-dry for 15 minutes.

2   Meanwhile, preheat the oven to 200°C (400°F) Gas Mark 6.

3   Add the goose fat to a roasting tray and place in the oven to heat up.

4   Once hot, carefully add the steam-dried potatoes with the garlic cloves and 2 whole sprigs of rosemary, leaving the stalks on. Spread the potatoes out, making sure they are all coated in fat.

5   Roast in the oven for 1 hour, turning with a spatula every 20 minutes, until golden and crisp.

6   Meanwhile, make the rosemary salt by mixing the ingredients thoroughly in a small bowl.

7   Using a slotted spoon, transfer the roasted potatoes to a large mixing bowl and sprinkle with plenty of the rosemary salt to serve.

FENNEL & PEACH SALAD

I am a huge fan of fennel and feel it isn't used enough in salads. The aniseed flavour, paired with the sweet peaches (make sure they are ripe and in season) and pesto dressing make this a wonderful side dish, or part of a spread.

SERVES 4 AS A SIDE

30g (⅓ cup) fresh breadcrumbs
1 tbsp olive oil
1 large fennel bulb
3 peaches

For the dill and walnut pesto
Large bunch of dill, leaves only
Juice of 1 lemon
1 tsp honey
40g (⅓ cup) walnuts, toasted
1 large garlic clove, peeled
4 tbsp olive oil

1 To make the dill and walnut pesto, add the dill, lemon juice, honey, walnuts, garlic, olive oil and a pinch of sea salt to a blender and blitz until smooth.

2 Add the breadcrumbs to a bowl with the olive oil and mix, then toast in a dry pan over a medium heat for 5–10 minutes until golden brown. Remove from the heat and season with sea salt.

3 Cut the top and bottom off the fennel bulbs, cut in half lengthways, then thinly slice.

4 Cut the peaches in half, twist to separate them, then remove the stone. Thinly slice each half.

5 Mix the fennel and peach slices in a bowl, pour over most of the dressing and gently mix together. Lay them out on a plate, pour over the remaining dressing and sprinkle the salty, crispy breadcrumbs on top to serve.

ROCKET, FIG & BURRATA SALAD

Burrata is one of the more luxurious ingredients, so make sure you eat it with the right things when you get it! The finishing touch of adding toasted pistachios and shaved Parmesan is key here, and makes the dish a wonderful platter to accompany most dishes. This is even great as a shared starter.

SERVES 3–4 AS A SIDE

½ tbsp honey
1 tbsp olive oil, plus extra for drizzling
Grated zest of ½ lemon
1 tbsp balsamic vinegar
60g (2¼oz) rocket (arugula)
15g (½oz) shelled pistachios
1 large ball of burrata
4 figs, tops removed, quartered
10g (⅓oz) Parmesan, shaved using a vegetable peeler

1 Mix the honey, oil, lemon zest, balsamic vinegar and a pinch of sea salt in a bowl. Add the rocket to the bowl and toss to combine.

2 Toast the pistachios in a dry pan over a medium heat for a few minutes until fragrant. Tip out onto a chopping board and roughly chop.

3 Lay the dressed rocket out on a platter, then tear open the burrata and place it on the rocket, in the middle. Lay the fig quarters around the burrata, then sprinkle over the Parmesan shavings and pistachios. Drizzle with a little more oil to serve.

QUICK KIMCHI-INSPIRED SALAD

This is a delicious accompaniment to any rich and meaty meal. Kimchi is a traditional spicy and garlicky fermented vegetable dish originating from Korea. This salad is a quicker interpretation of that, capturing some of the typical flavours without the extended fermentation process.

SERVES 4–6 AS A SIDE

2 tsp sesame seeds
2 garlic cloves, minced
2 spring onions (scallions), finely sliced
1 tsp dried chilli flakes
1 tbsp sriracha
Grated zest and juice of 1 lime
3 tbsp sesame oil
1 medium Chinese (Napa) cabbage, roughly chopped
1 pinch of gochugaru (optional)

1   Add the sesame seeds to a dry frying pan and toast over a medium heat for 5 minutes until golden and fragrant. Keep the seeds moving to ensure they do not burn. Tip onto a plate.

2   In a bowl, mix together the garlic, spring onions, chilli flakes, sriracha, lime zest and juice and sesame oil.

3   Add the chopped-up cabbage and give it a good mix to coat well.

4   Sprinkle with toasted sesame seeds and gochugaru to serve.

ROASTED SQUASH WITH SALSA MACHA

In my opinion, salsa macha is the king of all salsas. The smoky, nutty and spicy flavours make it incredibly tasty and versatile – it can go on almost anything. This recipe will make more salsa macha than you need, so store the leftovers in an airtight jar in the fridge for up to 3–4 weeks.

SERVES 4–6 AS A SIDE

1 large butternut squash
1 tbsp olive oil
1 tsp ground cinnamon
1 tsp dried oregano
4 tbsp sour cream

For the salsa macha
300ml (1½ cups) vegetable oil
6 garlic cloves, sliced
100g (¾ cup) peanuts
25g (2¾ tbsp) sesame seeds
6 guajillo chillies, deseeded and stalks removed
3 ancho chillies, deseeded and stalks removed
2 árbol chillies
1½ tbsp dried oregano
1 tbsp white wine vinegar

1 Preheat the oven to 180°C (350°F) Gas Mark 4.

2 Cut the squash in half and scoop out the seeds, then cut into slices 2cm (¾ inch) thick. Add to a roasting tray with the olive oil, cinnamon and oregano, season with sea salt and freshly ground black pepper and mix together. Roast in the oven for 45 minutes until caramelized and cooked through.

3 Meanwhile, make the salsa macha. Add the oil, garlic, peanuts and sesame seeds to a pan, place over a medium heat and cook for 6 minutes until the garlic starts to brown.

4 Once the garlic starts to change colour, add all the chillies and cook for another minute, then take off the heat and add the oregano. Mix, cover with a lid and leave to cool for 10 minutes.

5 Tip the salsa mixture into a food processor or blender, add the vinegar and a pinch of sea salt, then blitz until the nuts and chillies have broken down. Don't over-blitz – some chunks are nice for added texture.

6 Once the squash has roasted, spread dollops of the sour cream on a platter, top with the cooked squash and then drizzle over a few tablespoons of the salsa.

CHICORY, BLUE CHEESE & GRAPEFRUIT SALAD

Inspired by the use of bread in a panzanella, I wanted to create a wintery salad that still packed in the flavours. As with a classic panzanella, the longer you leave everything to sit, the better the salad gets. Over time, the toasted bread soaks up the juices, making each bite even more delicious.

SERVES 3–4 AS A SIDE

200g (7oz) ciabatta, cut into chunks
4 tbsp olive oil
½ tbsp honey
125g (4½oz) chicory leaves, cut lengthways into quarters
2 pears, peeled, cored and diced (190g/6¾oz prepared weight)
2 grapefruit, peeled with a knife and cut into segments (150g/5½oz prepared weight)
Handful of parsley, stalks removed, leaves picked
100g (3½oz) blue cheese

1 Preheat the oven to 200°C (400°F) Gas Mark 6.

2 Place the bread in a bowl with half the oil, season with sea salt and freshly ground black pepper, and mix well to combine.

3 Tip the bread into a roasting tray and cook in the oven for 10 minutes until golden and crisp. Remove from the oven and set aside to cool.

4 Combine the honey and remaining oil in a mixing bowl. Add the chicory, pears, grapefruit, parsley and toasted ciabatta chunks. Crumble in the blue cheese, then mix everything together until combined. Leave the salad to sit for at least 30 minutes before serving, so the toasted bread can soak up some of the juices and soften a little.

5 Check the seasoning and serve.

MISO AUBERGINE

Inspired by the Japanese dish 'Nasu Dengaku', I wanted to create a salad with miso aubergine that would be able to sit as part of any feast and stand out. Make sure to save some of the marinade to drizzle over the top of the dish at the end.

SERVES 4–6 AS A SIDE

3 large aubergines (eggplants), cut into large chunks
1½ tbsp sesame seeds
4 tbsp white miso paste
3 tbsp honey
Grated zest and juice of 1 small lemon
4 tbsp sesame oil
6 tbsp plain yogurt

1 Steam the aubergines for 5 minutes until softened, then remove from the heat and leave to steam-dry.

2 Add the sesame seeds to a dry frying pan and toast over a medium heat for 5 minutes until golden and fragrant. Tip into a bowl and leave to cool.

3 Preheat the oven to 200°C (400°F) Gas Mark 6.

4 In a small bowl, whisk together the miso, honey, lemon zest and juice and sesame oil, and season with sea salt and freshly ground black pepper. Remove one-third of the mixture and set aside to use later on.

5 Add the aubergine to the bowl of miso mixture and mix well. Spread it out on a roasting tray lined with baking parchment, then roast in the oven for 30 minutes, turning halfway through, until golden and crisp.

6 Once the aubergine has cooked, spread the yogurt on a plate, top it with the aubergine, drizzle over the remaining marinade and sprinkle with toasted sesame seeds to serve.

FOUR ESSENTIAL SIDES

This selection of sides are carb-based, very versatile and can be paired with a lot of different dishes.

BUTTERY-SPICED BASMATI RICE

SERVES 4

400g (14oz) basmati rice
½ tbsp cumin seeds
4 cardamom pods
40g (1½oz) butter
1 cinnamon stick
530ml (18fl oz) water

1   Tip the rice into a sieve (strainer) and rinse under cold running water for a minute. Completely drain then set aside.

2   Blitz the cumin seeds and cardamom pods together in a spice grinder or mini food processor until they form a fine powder.

3   Add the butter, cinnamon stick, and cumin and cardamom mixture to a saucepan over a medium heat. Melt the butter and toast the spices for 2–3 minutes until fragrant, then add the rice and mix together well so all of the rice is coated in the butter.

4   Pour in the water, add a pinch of sea salt, mix and cover with a lid. Bring to a gentle simmer over a medium heat, this will take about 4–5 minutes, then reduce the heat to low (the water should be very gently bubbling) and cook for 13–15 minutes until the rice has cooked through. Try to keep the lid on so the steam doesn't escape.

5   Once cooked, remove the lid, discard the cinnamon stick and fluff the rice with a fork to serve.

CHEESY POLENTA

SERVES 4

200g (1¼ cups) polenta (cornmeal)
530ml (2⅓ cups) whole milk
400ml (1¾ cups) water
70g (⅔ cup) grated Cheddar
50g (½ cup) grated Parmesan

1   Mix the polenta in a saucepan with the milk and water. Place over a medium-low heat and cook for 30–35 minutes until thickened, stirring constantly to ensure you get a smooth polenta.

2   Remove from the heat, add the grated cheeses, and season with freshly ground black pepper. Mix thoroughly before serving.

SERVES 4

SUSHI RICE

400g (14oz) sushi rice
400ml (14fl oz) water
65ml (2½oz) rice wine vinegar or
   white wine vinegar
25g (2 tbsp) caster (superfine)
   sugar

Note: Soaking the rice first helps maintain an even cook throughout the grains of rice; don't skip it!

1 Start by rinsing the sushi rice in water. Tip it into a large bowl and fill with water, then rub the grains between your hands for a minute, until it turns completely cloudy. Drain the water, refill with fresh water and repeat until the water is almost clear (it will never be 100% clear).

2 Drain completely, then tip into a saucepan and pour in the measured water. Bring to a gentle simmer over a medium heat, this will take about 4–5 minutes, then reduce the heat to low (the water should be very gently bubbling) and cook for 13–15 minutes until cooked through.

3 While the rice is cooking, make the rice seasoning by simply mixing the vinegar and sugar with a pinch of sea salt in a bowl.

4 Once the rice has cooked, remove from the heat, tip out onto a baking tray and pour over the rice seasoning while it is still hot. Gently mix it in using a spatula, making a cutting motion through the rice so you don't 'mush' up any grains. Serve or leave to cool, if being used for sushi.

SERVES 3–4

OREGANO & THYME FRIES

3 large white potatoes (such as
   Maris Piper) (880g/1lb 15oz),
   washed and cut into batons
   (1cm/½ inch thick)
3 tsp dried oregano
2 tsp dried thyme
3 tsp flaky sea salt
Vegetable oil, for frying

Note: After freezing, the fries can be tipped into a bag to save space and they will not stick together. These can now be stored until ready to cook. The freezing step significantly helps with drying them out and getting an incredibly crunchy, golden fry.

1 Place the potatoes in a bowl of cold water and wash them to remove any excess starch. Pour out the starchy water, then refill the bowl and leave to soak while you make the salt.

2 Grind together the oregano, thyme and salt in a pestle and mortar.

3 Drain the potatoes and dry with a tea (dish) towel.

4 Third-fill a casserole with vegetable oil and heat the oil to 160°C (320°F). Fry the potatoes in batches for 3–4 minutes until a light crust forms (we don't want any colour on the outside at this point). Remove them from the oil to a wire rack. When they are all fried, spread them out on a baking tray and place, uncovered, in the freezer overnight.

5 To finish cooking, heat the oil to 180°C (356°F), add the frozen fries, in batches, and fry for 4–5 minutes until crisp and golden brown. Remove using a slotted spoon, shake off any excess oil and place in a large bowl.

6 Sprinkle with the herb salt, toss together to fully coat, then serve.

TENDERSTEM BROCCOLI WITH TAHINI DRESSING

This side dish is simple but effective. It is a really easy way to level up your broccoli.

SERVES 2–3 AS A SIDE

Handful of flaked (slivered) almonds
200g (7oz) tenderstem broccoli (broccolini)
1 tbsp olive oil
1 large garlic clove, grated
Grated zest of ½ lemon

For the tahini dressing
1 tbsp tahini
3 tbsp water
1 tbsp plain yogurt
½ garlic clove, minced
Juice of ½ lemon

1 To make the tahini dressing, add all the ingredients to a bowl, with sea salt to taste, and mix. If the dressing is too thick for your liking, simply add a splash more water.

2 Add the flaked almonds to a dry frying pan and toast over a medium heat for a few minutes until browned. Tip out onto a plate and set aside.

3 Bring a pan of salted water to the boil and blanch the broccoli for a few minutes until softened. Drain and place in a bowl of ice-cold water to cool. Remove from the water and place on kitchen paper to dry.

4 Meanwhile, add the olive oil and garlic to a frying pan over a low heat and toast the garlic for a few minutes. Turn the heat up to medium, add the broccoli, then pan-fry for a few minutes until it starts to gain some colour.

5 Lay the broccoli out on a plate, drizzle with the tahini dressing, sprinkle over the flaked almonds and finish with a grating of lemon zest.

HERBY POTATO & CAVOLO NERO GRATIN

If it was up to me, I'd happily eat this all by myself as a main dish. However, for the sake of good health, serve it as the perfect side to accompany a feast. Who doesn't love creamy and garlicky potatoes?

SERVES 4–6

Large knob of butter (about 2 tbsp)

1 leek, cut into 5mm (¼ inch) rounds

2 sprigs of rosemary, needles finely chopped

5–6 sprigs of thyme, leaves only

2 garlic cloves, crushed

100g (3½oz) cavolo nero, centre stalks removed, leaves shredded

250ml (generous 1 cup) whole milk

300ml (1⅓ cups) double (heavy) cream

1 bay leaf

100g (3½oz) Gruyère cheese, grated

3 large potatoes (750g/1lb 10oz)

1 Melt the butter in a frying pan over a medium heat. Add the leek, rosemary, thyme and garlic, season with sea salt and cook for 5 minutes until softened, stirring frequently. Add the shredded cavolo nero and cook for 2–3 minutes until wilted.

2 Pour the milk and cream into the pan and add the bay leaf. Bring up to a gentle simmer and cook for 2 minutes, making sure it doesn't boil over. Take off the heat, stir in half the Gruyère, then cover and leave to sit for 5 minutes to infuse. Remove the bay leaf.

3 Preheat the oven to 180°C (350°F) Gas Mark 4.

4 Peel the potatoes and slice into rounds 1–2mm (¹⁄₁₆ inch) thick. If you have one, use a mandolin.

5 Place a single overlapping layer of potatoes in the base of a 24cm (9½ inch) diameter baking dish, or a rectangular one that is 18 x 24cm (7 x 9½ inch). Season with a good pinch of sea salt then spoon over some of the cavolo nero and leek mixture. Repeat the layers until all the potatoes and leeks have been used, then pour over any remaining liquid. Sprinkle over the remaining Gruyère and bake in the oven for 35 minutes until golden brown on top.

6 Leave to cool for a few minutes before serving.

SWEET TREATS

07

RASPBERRY SOUFFLÉ

If you are feeling like an extra treat, pair this with the homemade chai-spiced custard on page 221; you won't regret it. These soufflés are incredibly light and flavoursome, and are the perfect end to a meal.

MAKES 6

Butter, for greasing
Icing (confectioners') sugar, for dusting
4 large egg whites (about 160g/5¼oz)
1 tsp lemon juice
60g (¼ cup) caster (superfine) sugar

For the raspberry purée
700g (1lb 9oz) frozen raspberries
150g (⅔ cup) caster (superfine) sugar
1 tbsp lemon juice
Pinch of flaky salt
4 tbsp cornflour (cornstarch)
4 tbsp water

Note: Save the egg yolks to make custard (see page 221), homemade mayonnaise or add them to scrambled eggs.

1 To make the raspberry purée, place the raspberries, sugar, lemon juice and salt in a pan over a medium heat, and cook for 10 minutes. Remove from the heat and, using a hand-held blender, blitz for 15 seconds (no longer or the seeds will start to break up).

2 Strain the raspberries through a fine mesh sieve (strainer) to remove the seeds and place the smooth purée back in the pan. Mix the cornflour (cornstarch) with the water then add to the pan and mix. Cook over a medium-low heat for 5 minutes, until thickened and paste-like. Remove from the heat and leave to cool.

3 Meanwhile, preheat the oven to 160°C (325°F) Gas Mark 3. Butter the insides of 6 ramekins and lightly dust with icing sugar.

4 Place the egg whites and lemon juice into a large bowl and whisk on low speed until the eggs start to turn foamy with lots of miniature bubbles.

5 Gradually add the sugar to the egg whites, whisking all the time on medium speed. Once all the sugar has been incorporated, continue to whisk on a medium-high speed until stiff peaks form.

6 Add the cooled raspberry purée and one-third of the whisked meringue to a clean, large bowl and fold the egg whites into the purée until it is all incorporated. Add half the remaining meringue and fold again. Finally, fold in the remaining meringue. The mixture should be smooth and airy.

7 Scoop the soufflé mixture into the prepared ramekins (if you have a piping bag then this achieves a more even distribution), then shake gently to distribute the mixture evenly. Using a spatula (or any flat-sided tool), wipe across the top to leave the mixture flush with the top of the ramekin. Using your thumb, wipe around the inside edges of the ramekin to make a lip – this helps with an even rise of the final soufflé. Place the ramekins on a baking tray and bake in the oven for 19–20 minutes.

8 Remove from the oven, dust with icing sugar and eat straight away.

RICE PUDDING

Rice pudding is a British classic, so I was keen to include a recipe in this book. However, it wouldn't be me if I did it in the usual way! I absolutely love Thai mango sticky rice (*khao niao mamuang*) so, with that in mind, I have incorporated aspects of both dishes to create a very fulfilling dessert. The addition of passion fruit adds a lovely acidity that cuts through the richness of the coconut milk and the sweetness in the dish.

SERVES 4–6

250g (9oz) short-grain rice
350ml (12fl oz) coconut milk
750ml (26½fl oz) whole milk
Butter, for greasing
60g (¼ cup) caster (superfine) sugar
45g (1¾oz) stem ginger, finely grated, then squished to a pulp with the flat edge of a knife
1 small cinnamon stick
Pinch of ground allspice
Freshly grated nutmeg
30g (¼ cup) shelled pistachios, to serve

For the mango compote
1 ripe mango, flesh cut into small chunks
2 passion fruit, halved and pulp scooped out
50g (¼ cup) caster (superfine) sugar

1   Start by rinsing the rice under cold water, until the water runs clear, then place in a bowl, cover with water and set aside to soak for 30 minutes.

2   Meanwhile, prepare the mango compote. Add the mango, passion fruit and sugar to a saucepan, cover with a lid and cook over a medium heat for 25 minutes, stirring occasionally, until it has thickened to a jam-like consistency and the mango has softened. Remove from the heat and tip half the compote into a blender. Blitz briefly (not too much – you don't want the passion fruit seeds to break up), then mix it back into the rest of the compote.

3   Tip the coconut milk and whole milk into a lightly greased saucepan, place over a medium-high heat and bring to a bubble, making sure you don't let it overflow, about 5–7 minutes. Turn the heat down to medium-low, then add the sugar, ginger and spices, with a generous grating of nutmeg. Mix together until the sugar has dissolved.

4   Drain the rice then add to the pan of milk and spices and cook over a medium-low heat for 30 minutes, stirring frequently, until thickened and the rice has cooked through.

5   While the rice is cooking, toast the pistachios in a dry frying pan over a medium heat, then tip onto a board and roughly chop.

6   When ready to serve, spoon portions of the rice pudding into bowls, add some of the mango compote on top and sprinkle with chopped pistachios.

CHOCOLATE & PISTACHIO FONDANT

This chocolate and pistachio fondant is a very indulgent treat. If you are pushed for time, or want a cheaper alternative, you could make this without the pistachio filling.

SERVES 4

140g (5oz) dark chocolate (70%), broken into pieces
140g (5oz) unsalted butter, plus extra for greasing
Unsweetened cocoa powder, for dusting
2 whole eggs
2 egg yolks
50g (¼ cup) caster (superfine) sugar
1 tsp vanilla extract
40g (⅓ cup) plain (all-purpose) flour
Small pinch of fine sea salt

For the pistachio filling
90g (⅓ cup) caster (superfine) sugar
300ml (1⅓ cups) double (heavy) cream
160g (1⅓ cups) shelled pistachios
2 tbsp peanut or vegetable oil

Note: You will need 4 × 150ml (5fl oz) ramekins.

1 Start by making the pistachio filling (which needs to freeze). Add the sugar and cream to a saucepan and warm over a medium heat for a few minutes, until all the sugar has dissolved. Remove from the heat and leave to cool completely.

2 Add the pistachios to a dry frying pan and toast for 5 minutes over a medium heat until fragrant. Remove from the heat and tip into a food processor. Add the oil and blitz on high until smooth – this may take 5 minutes, depending on how warm the pistachios are. Stream in the cooled cream and blitz on high until completely combined.

3 Tip the mixture into ice-cube trays and freeze (it will take a few hours).

4 Once the pistachio filling has frozen, prepare the fondant. Add the chocolate and butter to a heatproof bowl and place over a gently simmering saucepan of water, making sure the water isn't touching the base of the bowl. Leave to melt, mixing to combine. (Alternatively, melt the chocolate and butter in a microwave.)

5 Preheat the oven to 180°C (350°F) Gas Mark 4. Butter the insides of 4 ramekin dishes, then sift cocoa powder lightly into each one to dust.

6 Using an electric whisk, beat the eggs and extra yolks together with the sugar until ribbons form (the beaters will leave a trail when lifted from the mixture). Use a large metal spoon to fold in the vanilla extract and cooled chocolate and butter mixture. Sift in the flour and salt, and fold into the mixture, being careful not to overfold the mixture and knock out the air.

7 Fill the ramekins half full, then place a cube of the frozen pistachio filling on top of each. Top each ramekin with the remaining chocolate mixture, then place on a baking tray and cook in the oven for 10–12 minutes for the perfect gooey centre.

8 Invert the ramekins onto serving plates, tap a few times to help release the fondant, then sprinkle with cocoa powder to serve.

GRANITAS

Granitas act as the perfect pallet cleanser after a rich meal. These also work as a delicious refresher during the hot summer months.

SERVES 10–12

1 x 400ml (14fl oz) can of coconut milk
4 tbsp sugar
350ml (1½ cups) water
Grated zest of 2 limes
Juice of 1 lime
Coconut rum, such as Malibu, to serve

COCONUT GRANITA

1   Add the coconut milk, sugar and water to a pan. Warm over a medium heat for 5 minutes, stirring continuously, until all the sugar has dissolved. Remove from the heat, stir in the lime zest and juice and leave to cool.

2   Once cooled, tip into a tray and place in the freezer for a few hours until completely frozen. Every hour that it is in the freezer, give the granita a mix with a fork.

3   Once frozen, scrape the top of the frozen granita with a fork until you have enough to serve.

4   Serve in small cold bowls and drizzle 1 teaspoon of Malibu over the top of each one (see bottom right on page 217).

SERVES 8–10

Large sprig of mint, plus extra leaves to serve
60g (¼ cup) caster (superfine) sugar
115ml (½ cup) water
3 cooking apples (325g/11½oz total weight)

APPLE & MINT GRANITA

1   Bash the mint on the work surface a few times to bruise the leaves and start the extraction of the oils.

2   Add the mint, sugar and water to a saucepan and bring to a simmer over a medium-high heat. Stir until all the sugar has dissolved, then take off the heat and leave to infuse in the fridge overnight to maximize flavour. Once ready, discard the mint stalks.

3   Peel the apples, remove the cores, and cut them into chunks. Place in a blender with the infused syrup and blitz until smooth.

4   Tip into a tray and place in the freezer for a few hours until completely frozen. Every hour, give the granita a mix with a fork.

5   Once frozen, scrape the top of the frozen granita with a fork until you have enough to serve.

6   Serve in small cold bowls with fresh mint leaves on top (see bottom left on page 216).

NO-CHURN

These two recipes highlight how easily you can make frozen desserts at home, without the need of any expensive equipment.

SERVES 6–8

350g (12oz) frozen strawberries
1 x 400g (14oz) can of sweetened condensed milk
600ml (2⅔ cups) double (heavy) cream
1 tsp vanilla extract
55g (2oz) digestive biscuits (Graham crackers), crushed into chunks

STRAWBERRY CHEESECAKE ICE CREAM

1 Place the frozen strawberries in a pan and cook over a medium heat for 10 minutes until softened. Tip into a blender and blitz until smooth, then add the condensed milk, cream and vanilla extract. Blitz again on high until combined.

2 Pour a third of the mixture into a loaf tin or plastic Tupperware, add half the crushed biscuits on top, then pour over another third of the ice cream mixture. Sprinkle over the rest of the biscuits then top with the remaining ice cream mixture to finish.

3 Place the ice cream in the freezer to completely freeze, about 4–6 hours.

4 Remove from the freezer 15 minutes before serving to soften slightly, then scoop out into bowls (see top left on page 216).

SERVES 4–6

8 peaches
2 tsp lemon juice
2 tsp water
3 tbsp honey
1 tbsp double (heavy) cream

Note: If you are not planning to serve this right away, it can be stored in an airtight container in the freezer. Remove from the freezer 30–40 minutes before serving, to give it a chance to soften a bit.

PEACH SHERBET

1 Halve the peaches and remove the stones. Cut into chunks and place in the freezer overnight, or until frozen.

2 Add the frozen peaches to a food processor with the lemon juice, water, honey and cream. Turn the food processor to high and blitz until smooth.

3 Scoop out into bowls to serve (see top right on page 217).

CHOCOLATE & CHERRY MOUSSE

Chocolate and cherries, a famous combination. This mousse is very light and can be served as a perfect sweet treat for those who love chocolate. Make sure not to leave out the biscuit crumb, as this acts as a great textural difference to the mousse.

SERVES 6

For the mousse
100g (3½oz) dark chocolate, broken into pieces
200ml (7fl oz) double (heavy) cream
3 large egg whites (about 120g/4½oz)
40g (3 tbsp) caster (superfine) sugar

For the cherry compote
400g (14oz) frozen stoneless cherries
40g (3 tbsp) caster (superfine) sugar
Juice of 1 lemon

For the biscuit crumb
5 digestive biscuits (Graham crackers), crushed
45g (3 tbsp) unsalted butter, melted

Note: Save the egg yolks to make custard (see page 221), homemade mayonnaise or add them to scrambled eggs.

1 To make the mousse, place the chocolate in a large heatproof bowl and heat the cream in a saucepan until it starts to bubble. Pour the hot cream over the chocolate and leave it to sit for a few minutes, then stir together until all the chocolate has melted and mixed into the cream. Place in the fridge to cool.

2 Meanwhile, place the egg whites in a bowl and whisk until frothy. Then, gradually add the sugar while continuing to whisk, until stiff peaks form.

3 Once the chocolate has cooled, add a third of the whites to the chocolate and fold them in – this first fold can be done with a little bit more force than the rest to make sure it is all combined. Fold in the remaining whites in two batches, until all combined.

4 Divide the mousse between 6 ramekins, then place in the fridge to chill for at least 4 hours until set.

5 Meanwhile, prepare the cherry compote. Add all the ingredients to a saucepan, cover with a lid and cook over a medium heat for 10 minutes. Remove the lid and cook for a further 10 minutes to reduce the liquid. Once reduced, tip everything into a blender and pulse until the cherries have broken down – don't blitz too much as you want there to still be some texture to the compote. Set aside and leave to cool.

6 To make the biscuit crumb, add the biscuit crumbs to a bowl with the melted butter and mix well.

7 Serve the mousse with some cherry compote on top, and a sprinkle of the biscuit crumb to finish.

CHOCOLATE ORANGE HOT CHOCOLATE

Hot chocolate reminds me of the times when we used to travel to Germany as a family for Christmas to see our cousins. We'd sip it while walking around the beautiful markets or on long walks in the snow. This recipe takes hot chocolate to a whole new level. The subtle hints of orange, nutmeg and cinnamon make this a winner during the cold winter months.

SERVES 4–6

930ml (generous 4 cups) whole milk
Freshly grated nutmeg
1 small cinnamon stick
Pared zest of ½ orange
50g (¼ cup) caster (superfine) sugar
90g (3½oz) 70% dark chocolate, broken into pieces, plus extra to finish
15g (1 tbsp) unsalted butter

1 Add the milk to a saucepan with a few good gratings of nutmeg, the cinnamon and strips of orange zest. Place over a medium heat for 5 minutes, stirring continuously and ensuring that it doesn't boil over. Once hot, take off the heat and stir in the sugar until dissolved, then set aside for 15 minutes to infuse – the longer this sits the stronger the flavours.

2 Add the chocolate and butter to a heatproof bowl placed over a pan of simmering water, making sure that the bottom of the bowl doesn't touch the water. Stir together until completely melted and combined.

3 Place the milk over a medium heat, remove the spices and orange zest, and warm it up again until hot. Gradually whisk the hot milk into the melted chocolate until it is all incorporated.

4 Ladle the hot chocolate into mugs and top with a grating of dark chocolate to serve.

MADE FROM SCRATCH

CHAI-SPICED CUSTARD

If you've ever visited India, you'll know the national love there is for chai, and it is for good reason. The mixture of flavours from all the different spices (especially the cardamom) gives chai its wonderfully unique taste. This custard takes those flavours to create a beautiful sauce that works with plenty of desserts.

SERVES 4–6

600ml (2⅔ cups) whole milk
1 cinnamon stick
10 cardamom pods, split open
4 cloves
4 slices of ginger
2 star anise
4 black peppercorns
40g (3 tbsp) caster (superfine)
   sugar
5 egg yolks
1½ tbsp cornflour (cornstarch)

1   Add the milk, spices and half the sugar to a saucepan and warm up for 5 minutes over a medium heat, stirring often to prevent the milk scorching on the bottom of the pan. Once hot, remove from the heat and set aside to infuse for 30 minutes.

2   In a large bowl, use a balloon whisk to beat together the egg yolks, cornflour and remaining sugar until pale and fluffy.

3   Once the milk has infused, discard the spices and reheat it over a medium heat.

4   Mixing constantly (but gently) with a balloon whisk, slowly pour the hot milk into the eggs. Once it has all been incorporated and is completely smooth, tip the custard back into the saucepan and place over a low heat. Cook, stirring constantly, for 7–8 minutes until the custard has thickened and is fully cooked.

5   Pour over a delicious crumble (see page 223) or a sticky toffee pudding (see page 224).

APPLE & PEAR CRUMBLE

Crumble is a quintessential British dessert and everyone has their own way of making it. For me, I like to cook and slightly mash some of the fruit, so there's a nice balance of compote and chunky soft fruit in the base. For the topping, pre-baking is essential to create a crunchy crumble that won't go stodgy and soggy.

SERVES 4–6

1 large Bramley or Granny Smith apple
5 large pears
115g (½ cup) caster (superfine) sugar
1 tsp ground cinnamon
Custard (see page 221 for homemade) or double (heavy) cream, to serve

For the crumble
150g (1¼ cups) plain (all-purpose) flour
40g (3 tbsp) caster (superfine) sugar
90g (1 cup) porridge (rolled) oats
120g (½ cup) cold butter, cubed
75g (⅔ cup) pecans, roughly chopped

1   Preheat the oven to 180°C (350°F) Gas Mark 4.

2   Peel and core the apple and pears, then cut into about 2cm (¾-inch) cubes. Place in a bowl with the sugar and cinnamon and mix together well. Tip a third of the fruit into a saucepan, and leave the rest in the bowl.

3   Place the pan over a medium heat and cook the fruit for 15 minutes until softened.

4   While the fruits are cooking, make the crumble. Add the flour, sugar and oats to a bowl and mix. Add the butter, then gently rub it into the dry ingredients using your fingertips, until the mixture resembles breadcrumbs (some clumps are nice here to give an extra crunchy topping). Mix in the nuts. Tip the crumble onto a baking tray and cook in the oven for 15 minutes until golden brown. Remove from the oven and set aside to cool.

5   Using a fork, mash the cooked fruit to break most of it up, then leave to cool. Mix the cooled fruit with the uncooked fruit, and tip all of it into a baking dish.

6   Spread the cooled crumble over the fruit in an even layer, place on a baking tray then transfer to the oven and cook for 45 minutes.

7   Remove from the oven and leave to stand for a few minutes before serving in bowls, with a generous drizzle of homemade chai-spiced custard (see page 221) or cream.

STICKY TOFFEE PUDDING

I had to include our family favourite – sticky toffee pudding with toffee sauce. This is the ideal way to end a Sunday feast with your friends and family. In my recipe the sponge is nice and light, so you won't feel like you've overdone it, which can often be the case with a heavy pudding.

SERVES 6–8

200g (7oz) pitted dates
100g (½ cup) light brown sugar
150g (⅔ cup) unsalted butter, at room temperature, plus extra for greasing
2 eggs
150g (1¼ cup) self-raising flour
Pinch of fine sea salt
1 tsp bicarbonate of soda (baking soda)
1 tsp ground cinnamon
¼ tsp ground ginger
100ml (3½fl oz) milk

For the toffee sauce
70g (⅓ cup) butter
300ml (1⅓ cups) double (heavy) cream
130g (4½oz) light muscovado sugar
40g (2 tbsp) black treacle (molasses)

1   Place the dates in a bowl and add just-boiled water to cover. Set aside.

2   Place the sugar and butter in a food processor and blitz on high until completely beaten together, then scoop into a large mixing bowl.

3   Crack both eggs into the bowl, then whisk until incorporated.

4   Preheat the oven to 160°C (325°F) Gas Mark 3 and grease a 24cm (9½inch) baking dish with butter.

5   In a new bowl, mix the flour, salt, bicarbonate of soda, cinnamon and ginger.

6   Remove the dates from the hot water, place into the previously used food processor and blitz to a paste. Tip this paste into the bowl of butter and eggs, and add the flour mixture and milk. Fold everything together until all incorporated, then tip into the prepared baking dish. Bake in the oven for 45 minutes. To check if it has cooked, poke a skewer though the cake and if it comes out clean, it is ready.

7   While the cake is cooking, prepare the toffee sauce. Add the butter, cream, sugar and treacle to a saucepan over a medium heat. Cook for 7 minutes, stirring continuously so the sugar doesn't burn. Remove from the heat and set aside.

8   Remove the cooked cake from the oven. Poke lots of holes in it using a skewer so the sauce can soak through the cake. Pour over two-thirds of the hot toffee sauce, saving the remaining third for serving.

9   Leave to soak for 10 minutes, then serve, or leave to soak for up to a few hours (if preparing in advance) and return it to the oven to reheat, before serving with the remaining sauce poured over.

US-UK CONVERSIONS

Below you'll find some common cup conversions, as well as the metric/imperial conversions. I always prefer to measure using metric scales, so following those quantities in the recipes will be the most accurate.

Weight Conversions

Grams	Ounces
10g	¼oz
15g	½oz
25/30g	1oz
55g	2oz
100g	3½oz
125g	4½oz
150g	5½oz
175g	6oz
200g	7oz
225g	8oz
250g	9oz
275g	9¾oz
300g	10½oz
325g	11½oz
350g	12oz
375g	13oz
400g	14oz
450g	1lb
500g	1lb 2oz
550g	1lb 4oz
600g	1lb 5oz
650g	1lb 7oz
700g	1lb 9oz
750g	1lb 10oz
800g	1lb 12oz
850g	1lb 14oz
900g	2lb
950g	2lb 2oz
1kg	2lb 4oz

Volume Conversions

Mililletres	Fluid Ounces
100ml	3½fl oz
125ml	4fl oz
150ml	5¼fl oz
175ml	6fl oz
200ml	7fl oz
225ml	8fl oz
250ml	9fl oz
275ml	8fl oz
300ml	10½fl oz
350ml	12fl oz
400ml	14fl oz
450ml	16fl oz
500ml	18fl oz
600ml	20fl oz
700ml	24½fl oz
800ml	28fl oz
1litre	35fl oz

Liquids

Spoons & Cups	Mililletres
¼ teaspoon	1.25 ml
½ teaspoon	2.5 ml
1 teaspoon	5 ml
1 tablespoon	15 ml
¼ cup*	60 ml
⅓ cup*	80 ml
½ cup*	125 ml
1 cup*	250 ml

These conversions hold true for water and many liquids.

Common Ingredients

Volume	Weight in Grams
1 cup butter	225g
1 cup plain (all-purpose) flour	120g
1 cup OO flour	106g
1 cup self-raising flour	113g
1 cup fresh breadcrumbs	85g
1 cup panko breadcrumbs	50g
1 cup granulated sugar	200g
1 cup icing (confectioner's) sugar	120g
1 cup grated Parmesan	100g
1 cup grated Cheddar	115g
1 cup long-grain rice	200g
1 cup old-fashioned oats	90g
1 cup sour cream	227g
1 cup vegetable oil	198g
1 cup whole walnuts	128g
1 cup water	227g
1 cup yogurt	227g

All cup measurements in this book are for US cups.

Oven Temperature

Gas Mark	Celsius	Fahrenheit
1	140°C	275°C
2	150°C	300°C
3	170°C	325°C
4	180°C	350°C
5	190°C	375°C
6	200°C	400°C
7	220°C	425°C
8	230°C	450°C
9	250°C	475°C
10	260°C	500°C

STORE CUPBOARD

Here are some store cupboard essentials that are used in recipes throughout the book. You don't need everything listed, but they are the ingredients I find myself using the most often.

Dried herbs
Oregano
Rosemary
Thyme
Bay leaves
Fennel seeds

Spices
Curry powder
Ground cumin
Cumin seeds
Ground coriander
Coriander seeds
Ground turmeric
Smoked paprika
Dried chilli flakes
Cardamom pods
Ground cinnamon
Cinnamon stick
Ground ginger
Garam masala
Kasoori methi
Nutmeg
Black peppercorns
Garlic powder
Mustard seeds
Cayenne pepper
Cloves

Sauces
Light soy
Dark soy
Fish
Worcestershire

Sweet chilli
Tabasco

Oils
Olive
Sunflower
Vegetable
Peanut (groundnut)
Sesame
Truffle
Ghee

Vinegars
Balsamic
White wine
Red wine
Rice wine
Apple cider

Condiments
Dijon mustard
Wholegrain mustard
Honey
Ginger paste
Garlic paste
Ndjuja paste
Tamarind paste
Rose harissa paste
Tahini
Sriracha
Mayonnaise
Chipotle paste
Gochujang paste
Peanut butter

Sugars
Caster (superfine)
Icing (confectioner's)
Brown

Pasta & Noodles
Orzo
Spaghetti
Pappardelle
Cavatappi
Rigatoni
Flat rice noodles
Macaroni

Rice, Pulses & Grains
Arborio
Basmati
Sushi
Red lentils
Chickpeas
Pearl barley
Quinoa
Polenta (cornmeal)

Cans
Chopped tomatoes
Coconut milk
Cooked chickpeas
Butterbeans
Kidney beans
Cannellini beans

Stock
Chicken
Beef
Vegetable

Dried Fruits & Nuts & Seeds
Medjool dates
Cashews
Almonds (whole and flakes)
Sesame seeds
Walnuts
Pecans
Pistachios
Peanuts

Flours
Plain (all-purpose)
Self-raising
Cornflour (cornstarch)
Masa harina
Tipo 00
Strong white bread
Semolina
Rice
Gram (chickpea)

Others
Sea salt (flaky, fine, truffle)
Panko breadcrumbs
Dried porcini mushrooms
Dried active yeast

KITCHEN EQUIPMENT

People can get lost in the sea of different kitchen equipment and utensils out there. If I had to recommend only two things, they would be a sharp knife and a high-sided frying pan or sauté pan with a lid. A quality knife will make cooking ten times more enjoyable as you slice through everything with ease, and it actually makes it safer. A deep frying pan or sauté pan with a lid can be used to cook almost everything.

However, as someone who has lots of different pieces of equipment in their kitchen, if you are ever looking to upgrade or want to know what else is worth investing in, here are the things I'd recommend.

Chef's Knife

As mentioned, a sharp chef's knife is the most important part of any home cook's equipment. Make sure it is sharp, as a dull knife is far more likely to lead to injury. They are practical for all types of chopping and are the most versatile of all knives. If you are looking for some specific knives to start out, pick a 'German-style' knife – they are durable and hold a sharp edge for a long time.

Stainless Steel Frying Pan

When I'm looking to get a good caramelization/ browning on food, I always resort to my stainless steel frying pan. The fact that they heat up quickly and spread the heat evenly, paired with the fact that they are uncoated, makes them the ideal pan for this. Searing steaks, browning minced (ground) meat for a ragù or stir-frying veggies are all great examples of when a stainless steel pan is best used. You'll need to make sure you use enough oil so nothing sticks and burns, though. Don't be afraid to add a little more than you think.

Blender

If there is one piece of electrical kitchen equipment I would recommend, it would be a blender. They help with so many different things, and it can be hard to replicate the process by hand. Whether you are making sauces, soups, dressings, marinades or smoothies, I find that a blender always has a role in my daily cooking. The cheaper alternative to a blender is a hand-held version; these are as effective and more compact.

Nonstick Frying Pan

The most common types of frying pan in shops are nonstick, and for good reason. I personally love to use a nonstick pan when it comes to cooking things that require only a little oil and, surprise, surprise, you don't want to stick. A prime example would be pancakes – a good nonstick surface makes a huge difference.

Heavy-based Casserole

Whether enamel coated or cast iron, one of these will always have a purpose in your kitchen. Slow cooking in the oven, deep frying and baking bread are a few times where they come into their own as they are very good at evenly heating and maintaining temperatures when cooking.

Heat-resistant Spatula

Whenever I'm cooking, I use one of these spatulas. They work in every aspect of cooking, can reach all the nooks and crannies in pans, are dishwasher safe and, most importantly, are very durable, so there's no need to worry about melting, warping or burning them. The brand Vogue are my go-to.

Fine Mesh Sieve (Strainer)

Whether you are straining peas or stocks, or smoothing out purées, a fine mesh sieve is an essential part of everyday cooking.

Chopping Boards

I use both wooden and plastic boards on a daily basis, for various tasks in the kitchen. Plastic are very helpful when preparing meat, as they can be placed straight in the dishwasher after use. Wooden chopping boards, on the other hand, stop knives from blunting faster, in my personal experience, so I use these as my day-to-day boards.

Measuring Cups, Jugs (Pitchers) and Spoons

Having a collection of measuring utensils is incredibly handy, and are used in all these recipes in some form or another.

Weighing Scales

A set of weighing scales is very helpful and would come in handy for most of the recipes in the book. Of course, cooking by eye is a great habit to get into. However, if in doubt, weighing and measuring ingredients beforehand is a safe way to cook the recipes well.

Microplane Grater

These are, without a doubt, the best graters of all. Microplane graters are incredibly useful for zesting citrus fruits, grating hard cheeses, grating garlic cloves and more. More so than a regular cheese grater, the angle of the microplane graters makes for a very efficient and effective grate.

Thermometer

This isn't a must, but I personally love to have a thermometer on hand, especially when cooking larger cuts of meat, or to ensure steaks are cooked perfectly every time.

Stand Mixer

All the recipes that involve dough and kneading in this book have been tested by hand, without the use of a stand mixer. But, if you have one, feel free to use it. They can be especially effective when paired with their various attachments, opening up a whole new world of home cooking.

Cheesecloth

Having some cheesecloth on hand can be very helpful when you are looking to get that extra fine strain on sauces and stocks, trying to squeeze out excess moisture from ingredients, or if you want to bundle up herbs into a bouquet garni.

INDEX

ACKNOWLEDGEMENTS

I never realised quite how monumental writing a book is. From the spark of an initial idea to the creation of a fully published book, a whole crew is needed. So, to every single one of you amazing people who have helped bring this book to life, thank you.

A big thank you must go to the team at Orion – Vicky, George, Helen, Nick, Jo, Helena, Frankie and the many others involved, as well as my agent, Carly – without whom, this book would not have been possible.

Thank you as well to David Loftus for the wonderful photography and for welcoming us all into his home for the photoshoot; Joss and El, who cooked and styled the food throughout the shoots, and to Louie for sourcing and selecting the beautiful props they used. A special thank you to all of you for making my first cookbook photoshoot an incredibly happy and positive experience – one which I will always look back on with a smile. It was the great company and endless laughs that turned what can often be seen as one of the most intense parts of the process, into one of the most memorable.

The biggest thank you goes to my family – Mum, Dad and my sisters, Lara and Hebe, thank you for the continuous support in helping me get to this point, I will always be grateful. And Hedy, my wonderful girlfriend, you have given me endless support, love and hours of your time – whether that was helping me tidy after long days of testing, giving honest feedback on recipes that did and did not work, and for keeping me grounded throughout this entire journey.

Finally, thank you to my followers. Without your love for what I do, I would seriously not be where I am today.

Sam x